CHRISTMAS IN NEW ENGLAND

AMY WHORF McGUIGGAN

CHRISTMAS IN NEW ENGLAND

*A Treasury of Traditions, from the Yule Log
and the Christmas Tree to Flying Santa
and the Enchanted Village*

COMMONWEALTH EDITIONS

BEVERLY · MASSACHUSETTS

ISBN-13: 978-1-889833-98-9
ISBN-10: 1-889833-98-3

First Edition

LIBRARY OF CONGRESS CATALOGING-IN-PUBLICATION DATA

McGuiggan, Amy Whorf, 1956–
    Christmas in New England : a treasury of traditions, from the Yule
  log and the Christmas tree to flying Santa and the Enchanted Village
  / Amy Whorf McGuiggan. —1st ed.
      p. cm.
    ISBN 1-889833-98-3 (alk. paper)
    1. Christmas — New England. I. Title.
  GT4986.N4M34 2006
  394.26630974 — dc22   2006011638

Cover design by John Barnett.
Interior design by Christopher Kuntze.
Printed in Canada.

Front cover: Traditional hand-carved Santa reproduced courtesy of SuperStock, Inc.
Back cover: James Van Alen, courtesy International Tennis Hall of Fame, Newport, Rhode Island.

COMMONWEALTH EDITIONS
266 Cabot Street, Beverly, Massachusetts 01915
www.commonwealtheditions.com

10 9 8 7 6 5 4 3 2

For Sophie, Colton, Mae, and Jack, who, like children of all ages, know the magic, mystery, and miracle of Christmas.

Contents

ACKNOWLEDGMENTS

To paraphrase a now well-known adage, it takes a village to make a book, and *Christmas in New England* is no exception.

First, my deepest gratitude goes to my publishers, Katie and Webster Bull, who took a suggestion I offered for a children's book and made it the starting point for this heartwarming treasury of Christmas stories. They saw the potential in this project even before I did, and their support and encouragement through the long months of research were invaluable. The care they take with every book they publish makes working for them a privilege.

I am grateful, too, to all the very able hands that shaped the book, particularly to the editor, Ann Twombly, and the designer, Christopher Kuntze. They were given the unenviable task of organizing more than fifty stories and one hundred images, but somehow married all the pieces into this beautiful, cohesive whole. *Christmas in New England* is a far better book than it would have been without their collective expertise and creative vision. Thanks, too, to John Barnett, whose cover design reminds us all of the simple charms of an old-fashioned New England Christmas.

This book could never have happened without the cooperation of the people across New England whose stories I have told. If, on occasion, we lose sight of the true meaning of Christmas, these stories will serve to rekindle our faith and to reassure us that the Christmas spirit is, indeed, alive and well. I thank all of these people who make Christmas special for so many others.

My thanks also to the librarians, curators, and archivists across New England who dug deep into their collections for the perfect photograph or illustration for our stories. We hope that the inclusion of so many rarely seen images will boost public awareness of the importance of historical preservation and appreciation for the extraordinary collections that New England institutions are fortunate to house. The individuals and institutions who so

generously contributed directly to this project include Jane Winton and the
Boston Public Library Print Department; Catharina Slautterback and the
Boston Athenaeum; Dover Publications; Michael Hillman; the American
Antiquarian Society; Hingham Middle School Home Economics Depart-
ment; Faith Ferguson and Follen Community Church; Maine Department
of Forestry; Nigel Manley and The Rocks Christmas Tree Farm; the Glessner
House Museum; Local 7 Ironworkers; the *Boston Globe;* Harron and Associ-
ates; Gary Castle and Nova Scotia Archives and Records Management; the
Connecticut Historical Society; Robert Dennis; Wilma Slaight and the
Wellesley College Archives; Mark Young and the International Tennis Hall
of Fame; Bob Smith; Dolly Snow Bicknell; Jeremy D'Entremont; Bob Can-
non and the United States Postal Service; Bill Connolly and Globe Santa;
Dartmouth College Library; A. O. Lucy and Believe in Books Literacy Foun-
dation; Monhegan Historical and Cultural Museum; Jake and Sparky
Kennedy and Nancy and Michael MacDonald; Kathy Carpano and Hasbro,
Inc.; Fred Wallace and the Framingham Historical Society; the Reverend
Stephen Cushing and New England Seafarers Mission; Jeffrey Smith and
Hallmark Cards, Inc.; Bethlehem, Connecticut, Post Office; Bethlehem,
New Hampshire, Post Office; Stacey Brooks and Strawbery Banke; Susanna
Bonta and Old Sturbridge Village; Michael O'Farrell and Mystic Seaport; H.
Flint Ranney; Ann Killen; Nantucket Chamber of Commerce; David Mar-
quis and Deborah Parkinson and ChemArt; Father Manuel Pereira and the
Reverend Donald Paradis, M.S., and LaSalette Shrine; the Bostonian Soci-
ety/Old State House; Anita Israel and the National Park Service/Long-
fellow National Historic Site; the Episcopal Diocese of Vermont; Stan Bevin
and Bevin Brothers Manufacturing; Chuck Kraemer; Radio Hall of Fame;
Robert O'Connell; Mary Jane Sawyer; American Guild of English Handbell
Ringers; Metropolitan Opera Archives; Hull Public Library; the Revels;
Lynn Van Dine; Boston Pops Orchestra; Mrs. Leroy Anderson and family;
Woodbury Music; Alfred Publishing Company; Jericho Historical Society;
Brooks Memorial Library, Brattleboro, Vermont; Vermont State Archives;
Archives of American Art/Smithsonian Institution; Tina Agren and Sab-
bathday Lake Shakers; Andrea Taaffe and the Shirley-Eustis House; Mrs.
Frances Raymond; Provincetown Public Library; Joyce Judge and the
Mayor's Office of Special Events and Tourism, Boston; Christian Hofmann
Company; Peter Cooper and Holy Trinity German Church; Helen Glover;
Roy Lauth; National Audubon Society; Massachusetts Society for the Pre-

vention of Cruelty to Animals; Roger Hall; Pilgrim Monument and Provincetown Museum; Julie Sopher and Shelburne Museum; Tom Kabelka and the *Republican-American*; Linda Grant and the Town of Farmington, Maine; Massachusetts Historical Society; Skip Whitson and Sun Publishing Company; the Parker House; Stockbridge Chamber of Commerce; Lynda Bronaugh and Redwood Library and Athenaeum. Many other individuals kept me pointed in the right direction and moving forward, and to them I am also indebted.

Last, but by no means least, I simply could not have seen this project through without the enthusiasm, guidance, and exceptional organizational skills of Jill Christiansen at Commonwealth Editions. When Webster teamed us up for this project it was as though I had found a kindred spirit. Her friendship is truly a gift. Merry Christmas, Jill!

I. Introduction

TRADITIONS connect us to one another and to our past. They tell us who we are—and were—and they give our lives meaning and memory.

Christmas in New England is a book about traditions. It is about the old ways that endure and the new ways that may someday be old. It is about once-venerated traditions that are, sadly, no more. It is about some of the people, places, and events that have helped to shape and define Christmas in New England.

New England does not necessarily have more Christmas spirit than any other region. Christmas, no matter where it is celebrated, is a day, a season, a pivotal time both to reflect and to look forward, a time to rekindle a child-like wonder and to see the world with new eyes. It is a time to "come home," both physically and spiritually, to become reacquainted with our loved ones and our traditions. It is a time to take stock, count our blessings, and share our surplus with others.

Still, there is a unique feel to a New England Christmas. It seems that no matter where one lives, everyone's Christmas is, at least in part, a New England Christmas. It is a cozy living room with a blazing fire, a piping mug of cider or hot chocolate and a plate of warm, spicy gingerbread boys and girls. It is woodlands of fragrant pine and an evening of crystalline air with a hint of wood smoke. It is the quaint, simple beauty of a town green and a white-steepled church aglow with candlelight. It is mittens and scarves, skating, sledding, and sleigh rides. And, most of all, it is snow.

Why has the old-fashioned New England Christmas become the quintessential Christmas? Perhaps it is our ancestral memory of the cold, dark pagan days of northern midwinter festivals. Or maybe it is that these New England shores welcomed many of the first settlers, who later spread out across the continent with a deeply ingrained sense of this place. Or is it that

New England's intellectual life, flourishing at the same time that Christmas was being embraced in New England, was best able to convey the sentiments of the season? What is certain is that our New England Christmas has its roots and traditions set deep in a time, long ago, when the only antidotes to the cold and dark were fellowship and forgiveness, generosity and goodwill. Not everything has changed. In some ways, very little has.

Pagan to Puritan

> And in that region there were shepherds out in the field, keeping watch over their flock by night. And an angel of the Lord appeared to them, and the glory of the Lord shone around them, and they were filled with fear. And the angel said to them, "Be not afraid; for behold, I bring you good news of a great joy which will come to all the people; for to you is born this day in the city of David a Savior, who is Christ the Lord. And this will be a sign for you: you will find a babe wrapped in swaddling cloths and lying in a manger." And suddenly there was with the angel a multitude of the heavenly host praising God and saying, "Glory to God in the highest, and on earth peace among men with whom he is pleased!"
>
> LUKE 2:8

CHRISTIANS, who date the birth of Jesus Christ to a December evening more than two thousand years ago, are often surprised to learn that his birth was a movable feast, celebrated on various days between December 25 and January 6, depending on the calendar used, for nearly four centuries. When the Church of Rome finally settled on December 25 for its new Catholic feast, there was scant historical documentation to justify the date. The Gospels, while detailing much about Christ's birth, never mentioned an hour, now fixed by tradition at midnight, or even a season.

So, why December 25 for a mass—an Old English word meaning feast—to celebrate Christ's coming? The simple answer is that a feast—and a season of celebration—was already taking place at that time of year.

Long before Christianity spread throughout Europe, ancient peoples across the continent honored the frosty, barren midwinter season with feasts and festivals. Daily life was entwined with natural seasonal rhythms, and the year, like an ever-turning wheel, was divided in half, between dark and light. The ancients perceived every turn of that wheel and imbued everything, living or not, with life. Gods and spirits were thought to control the elements

A Solstice Wish

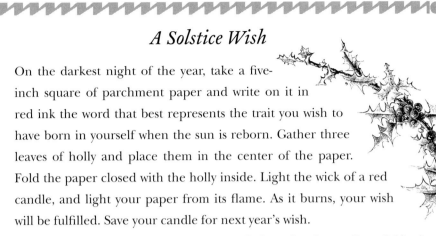

On the darkest night of the year, take a five-inch square of parchment paper and write on it in red ink the word that best represents the trait you wish to have born in yourself when the sun is reborn. Gather three leaves of holly and place them in the center of the paper. Fold the paper closed with the holly inside. Light the wick of a red candle, and light your paper from its flame. As it burns, your wish will be fulfilled. Save your candle for next year's wish.

Holly decoration. Courtesy Dover Publications.

and natural forces, and it was understood that certain times of the year were more mysterious and powerful, even more dangerous, than others.

The winter solstice, when the night is longest and the sun, the giver of all life, is at its weakest, was just such a time, a mysterious cusp of change and uncertainty. Folklorists, notably Sir James George Frazer (*The Golden Bough*) and Clement A. Miles (*Christmas Customs and Traditions*), tell us that the ancients, believing the sun was forsaking them, held great festivals of light, filled with ritual and symbolism, to coax the life source back to strength.

Pagan festivals could be raucous, hedonistic affairs filled with riotous merrymaking, goodwill, and forgiveness. Gifts were exchanged and homes were thrown open to friends. The ancient Romans called their festival Saturnalia, in honor of Saturn, their god of agriculture. Worshipped, too, by Romans was the Persian sun god, Mithras, *Sol Invicta*, the unconquered sun. In colder, northern climes, Scandinavians celebrated Jul (Yule), from the Norse word for wheel, *hweol*, and in Germanic cultures, great feasts celebrated the Twelve Nights. Central to all the celebrations, across all the European cultures, were the themes of hope, renewal, and redemption, the victory of light and life over dark and death.

Bonfires were kindled on hilltops. Animals, particularly the wild boar, a symbol of regeneration, were sacrificed and consumed in honor of Frey, the keeper of the herd in German and Scandinavian cultures. From grains, the main food crop, alcoholic drinks were magically fermented, symbolic of transformation. Confections were baked and ornaments made, symbols of the sun, moon, and stars, as offerings to the gods and goddesses.

Evergreens, with their mysterious ability to remain green and alive during the depths of winter, were brought into homes. So, too, with great ceremony, was the Yule log, a massive tree trunk that symbolized the bridge between the tree's branches in heaven and its roots in the netherworld. Originating in pagan Norse culture, where it was the embodiment of the Norse sky father, Odin, the Yule log was introduced to Celtic culture as Norse influence spread across Europe and the British Isles. Cut from the oak, the tree sacred to Celtic Druid priests, the long-burning log was first blessed and then set to smolder throughout the midwinter festival in an open hearth. A fragment, the brand, was saved and stored in the home to protect against lightning and illness. The brand was used to light the Yule log the following year. The log's sacred ash was gathered into amulets and sprinkled on orchards to increase yields in the coming year.

Lord of Misrule. From *Book of Days* by Robert Chambers, 1869. Courtesy Michael Hillman.

As Christianity spread across Europe, ancient heathen traditions and symbols were reshaped to meet the needs of the Roman Church, though much pagan superstition remained for centuries. Catholic saints replaced pagan gods and the celebration that once honored the birth of the *sun* now heralded the birth of the *Son*. Still, the medieval Christian celebration of Christmas was not unlike Saturnalia or Yule. Indeed, with the giving of gifts, the decorating of homes with evergreens, sacred fires, dancing, drinking, and feasting, Christmas was as boisterous and bacchanalian as any pagan affair.

Like Saturnalia, Christmas was an occasion when all people sat down together, freed from their societal roles to do and say what they pleased without fear of punishment. Roles were reversed and authority was mocked. It was an opportunity for the well-to-do to acknowledge their good fortune by providing for the less fortunate. In medieval England the festivities were led by a Lord of Misrule, a local peasant or beggar who served as the rowdy master of ceremonies. The Lord, modeled on the mock king from the Saturnalia, was to supervise the entertainment and maintain the nonstop merriment, revelry, and disorder. The festival became the occasion for elaborate theatricals and balls, sumptuous banquets, and fierce competition between kings and bishops upon whom noblemen and merchants lavished expensive gifts.

For Protestant reformers of the mid-1500s, the Christmas celebration, with its drinking, gambling, carousing, begging, and home invasions by costumed mummers, was all too pagan and materialistic. Martin Luther, convinced that the Church of Rome had become spiritually bankrupt, tried to discourage the celebrations, objecting not to Christ's mass but to how it was being celebrated. Despite his efforts and a return, in some places, to pious devotion, Christmas rowdiness and pagan revelry continued across Europe.

By the seventeenth century, another conservative movement, Puritanism, had spread across the British Isles. Christmas, denounced by Puritans as an abomination, a decadent, superstitious festival, was outlawed in the 1640s when Oliver Cromwell became lord protector of the commonwealth in England. The Puritans took their condemnation of Christmas even further than Luther. Unable to find authority for a specific feast day celebrating Christ's birth in the Bible, the Puritans condemned as sinful even the notion of a spiritual Christmas. But the Puritans, like Luther, could enforce the decree only so far. Custom proved more tenacious than law. Many resented Puritan authority and continued, in defiance, to keep the day, although not as publicly as they might have wished.

Mummers. From *Book of Days* by Robert Chambers, 1869. Courtesy Michael Hillman.

With the welcome restoration of the British monarchy in 1660, Christmas too was restored, though it would never again be the excessive and hearty public display of piping pipers, drumming drummers, leaping lords, gift giving, masquing, mumming, pageantry, procession, and all the other entertainments that it once had been.

New England Finally Takes a Holiday

IT WAS DURING England's Puritan reform movement of the seventeenth century that New England was settled by Puritan separatists—Pilgrims—fleeing persecution in their homeland. With an emphasis on moral earnestness and a strict adherence to Scripture, the devoutly orthodox Puritans condemned and ridiculed the celebration of Christmas, which they thought overshadowed the Sabbath.

From the Pilgrims' first footing on the bleak landscape of New England in 1620, December 25 was to be a common workday, a day like any other. In

Xmas

Xmas, the abbreviated form of the word *Christmas*, has been used since the sixteenth century, perhaps longer. The character X represents the Greek letter *chi*, the first letter of the Greek word for Christ. Xmas is not

Christmas postcard, 1910. Private collection.

an informal or disrespectful way to write Christmas, nor is it a subtle, modern attempt to take the Christ out of Christmas. Xmas should be pronounced "Christmas," however, and not, as the *Oxford English Dictionary* says, vulgarly as e·ksmæs

Mourt's Relation, a journal of the proceedings of Plimoth Plantation published in 1622 by G. Morton, Edward Winslow and William Bradford noted that on

> Monday, the 25th day, we went on shore, some to fell timber, some to saw, some to rive, and some to carry, so no man rested all that day. But towards night some, as they were at work, heard a noise of some Indians, which caused us all to go to our muskets, but we heard no further. So we came aboard again, and left some twenty to keep the court of guard. That night we had a sore storm of wind and rain.
>
> Monday, the 25th day, we went on shore, some to fell drink water aboard, but at night the master caused us to have some beer, and so on board we had divers times now and then some beer, but on shore none at all.

The following year, when an attempt was made by new, non-Puritan arrivals from the vessel *Fortune* to make merry in the streets on December 25, Governor William Bradford swiftly quelled the celebration. Like Luther, he seemed not to object to a solemn keeping of the day, but to its "joyful" expression and mockery:

> One the day called Chrismasday, the Governor caled them out to worke, (as was used,) but the most of this new-company excused them selves and said it wente against their consciences to work on that day. So the Governor tould them that if they made it mater of conscience, he would spare them till they were better informed. So he led-away the rest and left them; but when they came home at noone from their worke, he found them in the streete at play, openly; some pitching the barr, & some at stoole-ball, and shuch like sports. So he went to them, and tooke away their implements, and tould them that was against his conscience, that they should play & others worke. If they made the keeping of it mater of devotion, let them kepe their houses, but ther should be no gameing or revelling in the streets. Since which time nothing hath been attempted that way, at least openly.

Following the prohibitions on Christmas handed down in England during Cromwell's Puritan reign, the Colony and Province of Massachusetts Bay passed its own law in 1651 that imposed a sizable fine on anyone abstaining from work and "keeping" Christmas:

> For preventing disorders arising in several places within this jurisdiction, by reason of some still observing such festivals, as were superstitiously kept in other countries, to the great dishonour of God and offence of others:

Christmas in Boston (1889)

But first let me remind you that there were times when you could not have gone to any celebration in Boston, and there are those of us who remember when it would have been hard for you to find one. As late as 1700 or thereabouts, Judge Sewall was distressed almost beyond endurance at seeing the little wooden King's Chapel of that day open for public service. When I was a school-boy, I always went to school on Christmas Day, and I think all the other boys in town did. As we went home, and passed King's Chapel on Adam and Eve's Day, which is the 24th, we would see the men carrying hemlock for the decorations. But that was the only public indication that any holiday was approaching.

—Edward Everett Hale (1822–1909), *New England Magazine*, December 1889

It is therefore ordered by this court and the authority thereof, that whosoever shall be found observing any such day as christmas or the like, either by forbearing labour, feasting, or any other way upon any such account as aforesaid, every such person so offending, shall pay for every such offence five shillings as a fine to the county.

The Puritan governor interrupting the Christmas sports. Illustration c. 1880.
Courtesy Skip Whitson, Sun Publishing Company, Santa Fe, New Mexico.

Though the ban on Christmas was repealed in 1681, Puritans clung to political power and were loath, still, to recognize Christmas and its popish idolatry. By the early eighteenth century, dogmatic Puritan leaders were still thundering from the pulpit, as Cotton Mather did in a sermon on December 25, 1712, in opposition to Christmas: "Can you in your Conscience think, that our Holy Saviour is honoured, by Mad Mirth, by long Eating, by hard Drinking, by lewd Gaming, by rude Reveling; by a Mass fit for none but a Saturn or a Bacchus?"

If Puritans and their offspring—Congregationalists, Methodists, and Baptists—remained dogmatic, Anglican and Episcopalian settlers scattered throughout New England did not feel compelled to adhere to Puritan law. They continued to keep the day, quietly, with family. By the early nineteenth century, attempts had been made by various Protestant churches to provide for a solemn, public Christmas observance, but these efforts failed. New Englanders, with an anti-Christmas spirit deeply ingrained, had grown accustomed to treating December 25 like any other day.

The ultimate acceptance of Christmas in mid-nineteenth-century New England coincided with a number of dramatic social changes. The industrial and advertising revolutions, the influx of European immigrants who had all along been celebrating Christmas in their native countries, and improvements in communication and transportation that disseminated the idea of Christmas all contributed to the dilution of Puritan influence and helped to establish Christmas in the hearts and minds of New Englanders.

One by one the New England states recognized Christmas and declared December 25 a legal holiday—Connecticut in 1845, Vermont in 1850, New Hampshire in 1851, Rhode Island in 1852, Massachusetts in 1855, and Maine in 1858. In 1870 Congress declared Christmas a federal holiday, and Christmas as we know it was here to stay.

II. O Christmas Tree

SINCE ANCIENT TIMES, when vast primeval forests blanketed the land, man has worshipped trees as symbols of life and regeneration. Trees provide shelter, food, heat, tools, and clothing; the natural woodlands and groves were sacred temples. Few trees were more valued than the evergreen, honored for its life force and its magical ability to survive the rigors of winter. Ancient peoples used the fragrant boughs, symbolic of vitality and renewal, to decorate their homes during midwinter festivals. Early Christians adapted the evergreen, as they did so many pagan traditions, to satisfy the needs of the new church.

There is little doubt that our modern Christmas tree comes to us from Germany. St. Boniface, the Christian missionary who converted Germans to Christianity, is said to have witnessed Druid priests worshipping their sacred oak; when, in defiance, he cut down the oak, a fir grew from its root. The lighting of the tree is said to have begun with Martin Luther, the German Protestant leader of the Reformation. Inspired by a forest of evergreens, their triangular shapes pointing toward heaven, he felled a small fir, carried it home, and decorated it with wax tapers to mimic the stars shining through the branches—and to teach his son about Jesus, whom Christians call the Light of the World.

Americans may have had their first peek at a Christmas tree during the Revolutionary War when German mercenary soldiers, fighting for the British and stationed at Trenton, New Jersey, gathered around a Christmas tree in 1776. It was probably no coincidence that General George Washington, knowing that he might surprise the German soldiers who had abandoned their watch to celebrate the holiday, chose the dark evening of December 25, 1776, to cross the Delaware River to Trenton. In the years following the Revolution, German immigrants brought their Christmas tree tradition with them as they settled in Pennsylvania and the Midwest.

The Christmas Tree. From *Godey's Lady's Book*, 1850. Courtesy American Antiquarian Society.

The Christmas-Tree, by Winslow Homer. From *Harper's Weekly, 1858*. Courtesy Dover Publications.

With Puritanism deeply ingrained in New England, it would be many years before the region embraced the Christmas tree. New Englanders did not have their first public look at a Christmas tree until December 1850, when *Godey's Lady's Book*, one of the most popular and influential etiquette, style, and literary magazines of the time, published a scene of a family enjoying a Christmas tree decorated with candies, fruits, and small gifts. The illustration was a modified version of a drawing originally published in 1841 in the *London Illustrated News* depicting the British royal family, Queen Victoria and Prince Albert; the prince, homesick for his native Germany, had brought an evergreen tree to Windsor Castle. To appeal to a recently liberated people, *Godey's* removed royal references and added American flags to give the picture an American look. Enchanted by the intimate scene, Americans quickly embraced the evergreen.

The earliest American Christmas trees were communal, tabletop trees, "planted" and "dressed" in churches, where most families spent Christmas Day. Decorated with small, handmade tokens of gratitude, with pinecones, dried fruits, ribbons, gilded nuts, cookies, garlands of popcorn, tiny dolls and paper chains, the tree was the parish's gift to its children. As Christmas evolved into a domestic holiday centered on hearth and home, families put up their own trees decorated with family treasures. By the late Victorian era, the Christmas tree had become an elaborate display of gilded nuts, candies in cornucopias and eggshell baskets, tin soldiers, paper fans and chains, small penny toys, and newly available glass ornaments from Germany. Unveiled to the children on Christmas Eve, the "sugar tree" was meant to be a surprise, like a birthday cake. Its wax tapers were briefly lit—with buckets of water standing by in case of a conflagration—and its decorations eaten. The tree was then burned in the fireplace in ceremony.

President Franklin Pierce, a New Hampshire native, is often credited with introducing the Christmas tree to the White House in 1856, though no official White House record of a tree appears until the 1890s, during the administration of Benjamin Harrison. In 1895 another president with New England ties, Grover Cleveland, who summered on Cape Cod, began the tradition of decorating the White House tree with electric lights.

Burning the Christmas Greens. From *Harper's Weekly*, 1876. Courtesy Dover Publications.

Faneuil Hall Markets: A Merry Christmas. Courtesy Boston Public Library Print Department.

When, in 1901, the newly elected Theodore Roosevelt, an ardent environmentalist, chose not to put up a tree in the White House, thinking it would encourage the destruction of forests, the public outcry was proof that the Christmas tree had become a beloved and necessary symbol of the season.

American cities—Boston among the first in 1912—began putting up large Christmas trees on public greens and commons as symbols of community and fellowship, and in 1923 President Calvin Coolidge, a Vermont native, began the tradition of lighting a national community Christmas tree on the White House lawn.

Christmas Greens and Spices

THE POPULAR GREENS of Christmas came by their sacred status by an accident of nature. In northern climates, they would have been the only plants still alive—*ever green*—as planning for the celebrations began. The favorite Christmas spices were long known for both their medicinal and their perceived magical properties.

HOLLY

In Celtic mythology the Holly King, the masculine half of the sacred duo of plants, served as the lord of the old, waning year. As Christianity spread throughout Europe, holly became "holy" and lost its pagan associations. Holly's red berries were said to symbolize the blood of Jesus, and some believed that the cross on which Jesus was crucified was made of holly wood. Today, a sprig of holly hung over a doorway "catches" anything bad before it enters. A sprig on the bedpost snags bad dreams.

IVY

Ivy, the feminine half of the duo, was associated with the Greek god Dionysus, better known by his Roman name, Bacchus, the god of wine, revelry, agriculture, and fertility. The ancient Greeks crowned their poets with ivy; brides carried the plant as a fertility talisman. A climbing, evergreen vine that attaches itself to brickwork and trees, even dead trees, ivy became a Christian symbol of the soul's eternal life and the promise of new life. It has always been a more popular Christmas plant in England than in America.

MISTLETOE

There was no plant more sacred to the Druids than mistletoe, the "golden bough." Believed to have healing, even magical powers, mistletoe, a parasitic plant with no roots of its own, was thought to grow from the heavens and attach itself to the sacred oak tree, a symbol of strength, endurance, and nobility. The ancient Romans valued mistletoe as a symbol of peace and

believed that it could help end disputes. Christians banned mistletoe because of its association with pagan ritual, but many Christians continued to use the plant secretly because its magic was believed to be so potent.

ROSEMARY

Rosemary represents remembrance. The shrubby, aromatic evergreen was freely cultivated by the ancients, who used it to strengthen memory. Cast into graves and given to mourners, rosemary promised that the deceased would not be forgotten. During the Middle Ages, the plant was spread on the floor during festivals and ceremonies, where it released its pleasing fragrance as it was trod upon. As Christianity spread throughout Europe, rosemary was said to have received its divine fragrance when Mary laid the Christ child's clothes upon it.

CINNAMON

Cinnamon is one of the world's oldest spices, dating back more than seven thousand years. It was used in ancient religious services as incense, and medicinally as a curative for coughs and indigestion. Small sticks were exchanged as tokens of friendship between friends and lovers. True cinnamon, with its subtle flavor, grows only in Ceylon and India, and its exotic origins made it a status symbol in Europe. Cinnamon is a Christmas favorite, added to baked goods and to tea for a warming, soothing effect.

Cinnamon Holiday Ornaments

¾ cup applesauce   4 ounces ground cinnamon

Mix applesauce and cinnamon to form a stiff dough. Roll the dough on a cutting board dusted with cinnamon or between sheets of wax paper to ¼ inch thickness. Cut the dough with cookie cutters. Use the end of a straw to make a hole for hanging. Place on a rack to air-dry for several days. Turn occasionally. Hang with decorative ribbon. Makes 12–15 fragrant ornaments.

NUTMEG

The nutmeg tree is a large, tropical evergreen native to the Spice Islands (Moluccas) of eastern Indonesia. Nutmeg was long believed to have magical powers and was worn in amulets to protect against evil and danger. Now cultivated in Grenada, the spice is indispensable to Christmas cakes, eggnog, and mulled drinks. It loses its fragrance quickly; for best results, it should be ground from a whole nut immediately before being used.

LAUREL OR BAY

Laurel is a shrub or small evergreen tree native to the shores of the Mediterranean Sea. In ancient Rome, crowns of laurel were worn by persons worthy of distinction; from that tradition came *baccalaureate,* which signifies accomplishment (though one is always warned never to rest on one's laurels). Once used medicinally for rheumatism and headache, it was also placed in homes to protect against lightning. Today laurel is a popular seasoning for meats, soups, and stews and is used as a Christmas green primarily in roping and garlands.

Christmas Spice Cookies

3¼ cups all-purpose flour	1 cup margarine or butter
1 teaspoon baking soda	1½ cups sugar
1 teaspoon ground cinnamon	1 egg
¾ teaspoon ground ginger	2 tablespoons molasses
¼ teaspoon ground nutmeg	½ teaspoon finely grated orange peel

Preheat oven to 375°. Combine flour, baking soda, and spices. In a large mixing bowl, beat margarine or butter until soft. Add sugar and beat until fluffy. Add egg, molasses, and peel and 1 tablespoon water. Beat well. Gradually add flour mixture and beat until well mixed. Cover and chill for 2 hours or until easy to handle.

On a lightly floured surface, roll dough ¼ inch thick. Cut with cookie cutters. Bake on ungreased cookie sheet 6–8 minutes to desired texture.

Makes 50–100 cookies, depending on size.

—Recipe courtesy Hingham Middle School Home Economics Department

GINGER

To aid digestion, the Greeks ate a piece of ginger wrapped in bread after a meal. By the Middle Ages ginger, thought to have come originally from the Garden of Eden, was used as a spice to cover food spoilage and as a key ingredient in gingerbread, a delicacy made only by baker's guilds and sold throughout the year at European fairs. Stamped with designs and cut into symbolic shapes associated with the seasons, gingerbread became a staple of Christmastime, the only time of the year when everyone was permitted to bake the costly and exotic confection. Ginger ale is still used today to settle an upset stomach. Gingerbread has become a traditional Christmas treat, baked in the shape of boys and girls and used to construct elaborate, candied Hansel and Gretel houses.

Charles Follen and the Christmas Tree Church

IN HIS NATIVE GERMANY, Charles Follen was a fearless advocate for social justice, railing against despotism. As a political refugee in America, the radical Follen continued to espouse republican principles and became a passionate, often strident voice in the abolitionist movement. Today, though, he may best be remembered as the man who brought the Christmas tree to New England.

Born into an elite family in Hesse-Darmstadt, Germany, in 1796, Charles early on immersed himself in student politics in the years following the French Revolution. After being arrested for his alleged role in a political murder, for which he was acquitted, Follen was looked upon with suspicion by German authorities. Persecuted, he was forced to flee the country, traveling to France and Switzerland, where he spent several years in exile.

Follen Church. Courtesy Follen Community Church, Lexington, Massachusetts.

By late 1824, with a letter of introduction from Lafayette, Charles had arrived in America; in 1825 he was offered a position at Harvard teaching the first courses in German and gymnastics. Invigorated by the freedoms that America offered, Charles continued his work on behalf of the oppressed. His magnetic personality, keen intellect, and uncompromising commitment to democratic ideals won him friends among Boston's intellectuals, but he

THIS TREE
was purchased from
"The
Christmas
Tree
Church"

In 1832 Dr. Charles
Follen, first minister
of Follen Community
Church, introduced
the Christmas Tree
custom to America.

Follen Community Church
755 Mass. Ave., Lexington

Christmas tree tag. Courtesy Follen Community Church, Lexington, Massachusetts.

made enemies among those who believed he threatened the status quo. In 1828 he married Eliza Lee Cabot, of the well-to-do Boston Cabots, and through Eliza he befriended William Ellery Channing, a prominent Unitarian minister with whom he pursued divinity studies and became immersed in the antislavery movement.

In 1830 Charles and Eliza had a son, little Charley, for whom Follen revived a tradition from his own German childhood. In her biography of Follen, *Life of Charles Follen*, published in 1842, after his death, Eliza wrote that though Charles's childhood was not particularly happy, he had fond memories of the family Christmas tree:

> One of the pleasures of his boyhood, that he loved best to remember, was the Christmas-tree, which, in his father's family, as is almost the universal custom in Germany, was prepared every Christmas eve for the children. He well remembered, he has told me, his joy, when he saw the pretty, well proportioned evergreen tree carried into the drawing-room,

into which, after that time, no child was to enter unbidden, and the holy mystery with which it was invested. . . .

Every Christmas since Charles was two years old, his father had dressed a Christmas-tree for him, after the fashion of his own country. This was always the happiest day in the year to him. He spared no pains, no time, in adorning the tree, and making it as beautiful as possible. This year he went himself into the woods with Charles and his pupils, and selected a fine spruce tree, and spent many hours preparing it, and cutting ornaments for it of different colored paper, & c. Every one in the family contributed to its decoration. Then he placed waxed tapers on every branch, carefully, so as to light the tree perfectly, but not to set fire to anything.

But for a houseguest who wrote about the celebration, Follen's decorated tree might never have been more than a quiet family tradition. Harriet Martineau, an English journalist and Unitarian who was visiting Boston to add her voice to the abolitionist chorus, recalled the magical scene at the Follens' Cambridge home:

I was present at the introduction into the new country of the spectacle of the German Christmas Tree. My little friend Charley (Follen's son) and three companions had long been preparing for this pretty show. The cook had broken eggs carefully in the middle for some weeks past, that Charley might have the shells for cups; and these cups were gilded and colored very prettily. We were all engaged in sticking on the last seven dozen of wax tapers, and in filling the gilded egg cups and gay paper cornucopias with comfits, lozenges and barley sugar. The tree was the top of a young fir, planted in a tub which was ornamented with moss. Smart dolls and other whimsies glittered on the evergreen and there was not a twig which had not something sparkling upon it.

It really looked beautiful; the room seemed in a blaze, and the ornaments were so well hung on that no accident happened, except that one doll's petticoat caught fire. There was a sponge tied to the end of a stick to put out any supernumerary blaze, and no harm ensued.

I mounted the steps behind the tree to see the effect of opening the doors. It was delightful. The children poured in, but in a moment every voice was hushed. Their faces were upturned to the blaze, all eyes wide open, all lips parted, all steps arrested. Nobody spoke, only Charley leaped for joy. The first symptom of recovery was the children's eyes wandering around the tree. At last a quick pair of eyes discovered that it bore something eatable and from that moment babble began again. . . . I have little doubt that the Christmas tree will become one of the most flourishing exotics of New England.

By 1835 Charles's unwillingness to moderate his radical antislavery position, a position that made even Northerners uncomfortable, had cost him tenure at Harvard. He began lecturing and preaching and later that same year received an invitation to preach to a small congregation in East Lexington. When a more lucrative position at All Soul's Church in New York was offered, Charles resigned his position in East Lexington, arranging for his friend Ralph Waldo Emerson to succeed him. By 1839 he had fallen out of favor with the church establishment in New York, again over the issue of abolition, and he was back in East Lexington making plans for a new church to be built.

Designed by Follen, the church would be octagonal, with curved pews, so that the minister would be among and not above his congregation. Ground was broken on July 4, 1839, and in his remarks Follen expressed his hope that the church doors would be open to everyone, particularly those who championed the cause of the oppressed: "May this new church never be desecrated by intolerance or bigotry. May its doors never be closed against any one who would plead in it the cause of oppressed humanity. We pray that within its walls all unjust and cruel distinctions might cease, and that here all might meet as brethren."

In her *Life of Charles Follen*, Eliza remembered her husband's plans for the new church:

> His great object was to produce a more truly social worship; he wished that the congregation should take an active part in the services, particularly in the devotional parts. He wished to see a closer union between members of the same church, to bring the minister more among the people. He wished to do away with the high pulpit, to have the building so constructed so that whoever desired to speak could easily find a place to stand, where he could be heard by the whole audience.

Construction progressed smoothly and a dedication was set for January 15, 1840.

Sadly, Charles never saw his church dedicated. Called away to New York for a series of lectures, he was returning to Lexington aboard the SS *Lexington* on January 13 when it caught fire and sank off Eaton's Neck in Long Island Sound. It may have been a coincidence that Follen was aboard the *Lexington,* but it was a sad irony that the fire had been started by bales of southern cotton packed around the ship's smokestack.

William Ellery Channing eulogized his friend as one whose "countenance, which at times wore a stern decision, was generally lighted up with a beautiful benignity; and his voice which expressed, when occasion required it, an inflexible will, was to many of us musical beyond expression, from the deep tenderness which it breathed."

In 1885 the East Lexington congregation adopted the name Follen for its church. Every year the church—the oldest church building in Lexington and now fondly known as the Christmas Tree Church—pays tribute to Charles Follen's legacy of social activism and community service and his inherent belief in the dignity of all people by selling Christmas trees to raise money for church and social outreach programs. His life of purpose and meaning is remembered in Christmas sermons. A former minister there, the Reverend Polly Guild, remarked that "another reason to speak of the Follens in connection with Christmas is that their lives exemplified the Christmas message. Though full of sadness, disappointment, and despair, their lives are remembered most for joy, light, and cheer which they brought out of the darkness."

The Follen Church is on the National Register of Historic Places.

Tipping the "Tree of Life"

WAY DOWN EAST, in Maine, where day first breaks in the United States and Christmas arrives before it does anywhere else in the country, fragrant balsam fir perfumes the air. Imagine Christmas—or Maine—without that irresistible, resinous aroma. A member of the pine family, the balsam fir (*Abies balsamea*) is Maine's most abundant conifer and the pine of choice when it comes to Christmas trees and holiday decorating.

It used to be that only Northerners could enjoy a fresh tree during the Yuletide, but then grand sailing schooners began calling at ports in Maine, taking on cargoes of pine trees, and delivering them south along the coast. Now modern transportation makes it possible for folks all over the country, indeed the world, to have not only a fresh tree, but a fresh *Maine* tree.

The demand today for fresh greenery during the Christmas season has more and more Mainers taking to the woods, as they have for generations, to gather by hand the fragrant greens for wreaths, swags, garlands, and kissing balls. They are known as "tippers" or "brushers," and in early November, with clippers, ladders, axes, and baler twine in hand, these hardy Mainers awake early and head out into the chilly, still-dark morning of Hancock and Washington counties. Down lonely dirt roads, deep into the Maine woods they trudge, carefully snipping or snapping off the tips, or ends, of balsam fir branches. Mother nature has to cooperate. The tips, also known as brush,

Selling wreaths at Quincy Market, c. 1950. Courtesy Boston Public Library Print Department.

Wagonload of Christmas trees, Hartford, Connecticut, c. 1890. Courtesy Connecticut Historical Society.

Christmas trees at Faneuil Hall, 1956. Courtesy Boston Public Library Print Department.

can be collected only if there have been two or three hard frosts (twenty de-grees or colder) to form the waxy coating that seals the pores and hardens the blunt-ended needles onto branches. An early snow, insulating the tips against frost, can disrupt the whole delicate process.

Most tippers begin their work by cutting down a small tree, four to six feet tall, and stripping its trunk of all branches except its bottom whorl. What re-mains is the "stick," onto which the tips, measuring twelve to twenty inches and cut from surrounding trees, are stacked in alternating directions. Once the stick is full, it is wrapped and secured with twine. A completed stick of brush can weigh as much as a hundred pounds; attaching twine at both ends of the stick to form a shoulder strap makes it easier to carry. An aver-age tipper can collect as much as five hundred pounds in a day. The harvest continues until mid-December, when the demand for holiday greens subsides.

Only the highest-quality tips, dark green and round with flexible, robust needles on all sides (sometimes called bottlebrush tips), and with no evidence of insect damage, will do. The best tips are those from the middle of the tree on its sunny side. Collected properly, from trees at least ten feet tall and from no more than one-third of the tree, tips are a renewable resource, regenerating within three years.

Start a Yule Log Tradition

To make a Yule log from a Christmas tree, remove all the branches and cut the tree trunk into several small lengths that will fit into a fireplace, woodstove, or patio chiminea. Set one log aside to dry until the following Christmas Eve, when it will be lit. Do not allow the wood to burn completely; save a brand for the lighting of next year's log. Gather the ashes from the burned Yule log and scatter them in the garden or on trees.

The Yule Log. From *Book of Days* by Robert Chambers, 1869. Courtesy Michael Hillman.

Countless Maine families have passed on the art of tipping from parent to child. Whether one is delivering sticks of brush to one of Maine's wreath wholesalers or retailers or wrapping bundles of brush onto wire frames at one's own kitchen table, the harvesting of balsam fir has become an important cottage industry that provides seasonal employment to supplement and diversify rural incomes—not to mention seasonal enjoyment the world over!

The Rocks Estate Christmas Tree Farm

DEEP IN THE MOUNTAINS of New Hampshire, between the Old Man in the Mountain (or where he used to be) and majestic Mount Washington, at the highest township east of the Rockies, lies the picturesque village of Bethlehem, the Star of the White Mountains. Once a traditional hunting ground of the native Abenakis, the area saw its first permanent settlement in 1787. The village became a thriving farm town, and on December 25, 1799, the last Christmas of the century, it was incorporated as the town of Bethlehem.

Sawmills and gristmills later dotted the landscape, but by the late nineteenth century, tourists and hay fever sufferers had discovered Bethlehem, flocking to the town and its more than thirty grand hotels on Main Street, especially during the summer months, to take in Bethlehem's fresh, pollen-free mountain air and scenic views.

One of those summer visitors was John Jacob Glessner, a prominent Chicago captain of industry and a philanthropist. As a founder of the farm machinery company International Harvester, Glessner had been an innovator in farm technologies, and in 1882 he purchased a tract in Bethlehem, which he named The Rocks for its many glacial boulders, as a summer retreat and farm. Here he experimented with state-of-the-art equipment and implemented innovative approaches to forestry and agriculture. By the turn of the twentieth century, Glessner's estate had grown to two thousand acres. With a fine dairy herd, hayfields, acres of second-growth forest, stone walls built by Italian masons, formal, Olmsted-designed gardens, and architecturally significant farm buildings, The Rocks was one of the most prestigious properties of its day.

In 1978 Glessner's grandchildren donated the estate to the Society for the Protection of New Hampshire Forests. Founded in 1901 to protect the state's most important landscapes and to encourage wise use of renewable resources, the society counted Glessner as one of its first members. Grateful to be entrusted with stewardship of the property, the society, which today owns 145 properties and protects a million acres across the state, was bound by the stipulation set out in the donation agreement that The Rocks always maintain a crop. At the time of the dona-tion, the property was being leased by a dairy farmer growing grass and hay. When that lease expired, the society worked with the Glessner family, who agreed that grow-ing Christmas trees satisfied the agreement. In the late 1980s the first trees were planted and in 1995 the first mature trees were har-vested. Today more than seven thousand seedlings are planted each year and five thousand trees are harvested; the proceeds

John Jacob Glessner. Courtesy Glessner House Museum, Chicago.

help to support land protection, education, and advocacy programs.

Open to the public for selection and harvesting from Thanksgiving to Christmas Eve, The Rocks partners with more than twenty local hotels, inns, and bed-and-breakfasts to offer families an old-fashioned "Northern Rock-well" experience, complete with horse-drawn wagon rides, a wreath, and the perfect Rocks balsam—what the society boasts is the ultimate conservation tree, a tree grown on protected land by an organization dedicated to land protection and wise use.

A visit to The Rocks, with its majestic, panoramic views of the White Mountains, resident populations of deer, fox, and moose, miles of stone walls, historic farm buildings, hiking and snowshoeing trails, and an air redolent with balsam, has become a cherished Christmas tradition for New Englanders seeking the same respite and rejuvenation as visitors did a cen-tury ago.

Topping Off

THERE COMES A TIME in the life of every American office building, church, museum, college dormitory, town hall, city hall, any building made of a steel skeleton, when the final beam, the highest beam, of the skeletal frame is ready to be swung into place. Before being hoisted aloft, the beam is signed by everyone who worked on the project. The Stars and

Stripes are anchored to one end of the beam, an evergreen tree to the other, and then up it goes to the connectors. Though there is still much work to be done on the building, the "topping off" represents a significant milestone in the construction process.

But why an evergreen tree to top the building? The tradition is said to have come to America with Norwegian ironworkers in the late 1890s, though topping off dates to a much earlier time, when ancient Scandinavians crowned their communal houses with a sheaf of wheat to honor Sleipnir, the mighty eight-legged steed of the supreme Norse god, Odin. Odin would, in turn, bestow good fortune on the home.

Over time the sheaf of wheat for Sleipnir was replaced by an evergreen, symbolic of the life force and a sacred emblem of the Norse Yule celebration. Today, if the ancient folklore has been forgotten, the sentiment has not. The topping-off ceremony is a cherished tradition among ironworkers, no matter what the season. The tree is a symbol of hope, hope that life in the new building will prosper and that good luck will carry over to the next project.

The Gift of Green: The Halifax Explosion

THE YEAR WAS 1917 and war was raging in Europe. In the city of Halifax, Nova Scotia, fishing boats, ferries, and wartime shipping crowded the deep, natural, protected harbor. As a staging port for transatlantic convoys, the city was a bustling hub of activity. New rail lines had been completed, the economy was robust, and employment opportunities were plentiful. As December 6 dawned crisp and clear, Halifax was a city of promise. No one could have imagined the disaster that was about to befall it.

The French vessel *Mont Blanc*, loaded with munitions and preparing to cross the U-boat–infested Atlantic, had steamed north from New York to join a convoy in Halifax's Bedford Basin. To avoid detection by enemy eyes, the ship was not flying the flag that identified it as a munitions ship. Having arrived late in Halifax, after submarine nets had sealed off the harbor, the *Mont Blanc* spent the night outside the harbor. Early on the morning of December 6 it weighed anchor and began to steam in.

At the same time, the Norwegian vessel *Imo* was departing the Bedford Basin on its way to New York to take on a cargo of relief supplies for Belgium. A succession of misjudged and ill-timed maneuvers put the two vessels on a collision course. The *Imo* struck the *Mont Blanc*, and though the impact did not badly damage the ship, it did spark a fire aboard the *Mont Blanc,* whose decks and holds, unbeknown to spectators, were loaded with picric acid, TNT, guncotton, and benzol.

The crew of the *Mont Blanc,* anticipating an explosion, launched the vessel's lifeboats and rowed frantically across the narrows of the harbor toward the nearby Dartmouth shore. Their desperate warning cries, in French, went unheeded as the ship drifted toward Pier 6 at the north end of Halifax.

For twenty minutes the *Mont Blanc* burned, enough time for hundreds to flock to the waterfront to watch the spectacle. And then, with horrific consequences, the ship exploded, the largest man-made explosion before the detonation of the atomic bomb. So catastrophic was the explosion that not a single piece of the *Mont Blanc* remained.

Three hundred twenty-five acres of Halifax were leveled by the cataclysmic blast that sent a white cloud of smoke billowing 20,000 feet into the sky. More than 1,500 people were killed, 250 of whom were never identified; 9,000 were injured, many blinded by shattering glass, and 6,000 were left homeless. Hundreds of the dead were children. More than 13,000 homes, apartments, and businesses were damaged or destroyed. Fifty miles away, windows shattered; shock waves were felt throughout Nova Scotia. In Halifax, well-stocked winter supplies of coal and wood only stoked the raging fires. A tidal wave from the blast claimed more lives. And if the people of Halifax were not bewildered enough, a winter blizzard that evening left the devastated city under a foot of snow.

Mercifully, the city's large contingent of wartime troops and ships enabled relief efforts to begin immediately. Word spread quickly and assistance flowed in from other parts of Nova Scotia and New Brunswick. Within hours, word of the tragedy had reached Boston and by evening a "rescue train" was on its way to Halifax, carrying Harvard doctors and surgeons, nurses, medical supplies, social workers, building supplies, food, blankets, money, and other volunteers, regular working people who left their own jobs and families to assist with the relief efforts. Many stayed on in Nova Scotia for months and became part of the rebuilding effort.

In time, Halifax rose from the ashes, but the city never forgot the unstinting and continued generosity and goodwill of Bostonians. In 1971 the people of Halifax sent Boston a Christmas tree, and every year since a magnificent forty-foot white spruce from one of Nova Scotia's old-growth forests is cut and shipped to Boston. For years the tree stood, strung with the light and hope of the season, at Boston's Prudential Center. Now Boston's "Official Christmas Tree" graces Boston Common as the centerpiece of Boston's annual holiday tree lighting on Boston Common. When the mayor switches on the tree's lights in early December, Boston's holiday season officially begins.

Most of the survivors of the Halifax explosion are gone now, but the disaster of December 6, 1917, will forever live in the soul of the city. Every December 6, at 9:00 A.M. in Halifax, bells ring in memory of the victims. Bostonians, too, remember, and with Halifax's annual gift of green, they share not only the city's grief, but also its spirit of rebirth.

The visit of Governor Samuel McCall (second adult from left) of Massachusetts to Halifax, Nova Scotia, in 1918, on the first anniversary of the explosion that rocked that city. Courtesy Nova Scotia Archives and Records Management, Halifax.

Merry Old Santa Claus, by Thomas Nast. From *Harper's Weekly*, 1881.
Courtesy Dover Publications.

III. St. Nicholas

LIKE SO MANY of our Christmas traditions, Santa Claus has his origins in ancient times.

For the pagan peoples of Europe, the world was in an eternal struggle between light and dark. To reconcile that struggle and keep the world safe, the Celts had their Oak and Holly Kings, two aspects of the same being. The Oak King ruled from the winter solstice until the summer solstice, the Holly King from the summer solstice until the winter solstice. Representing the cycle of the year, the Oak King, in the guise of the robin, was the child of promise, the waxing year; the Holly King, in the guise of the wren, was the god of death, the waning year. The Holly King, in red and green and attended by sacred deer and nature sprites, brought respite to the world, quieting souls for the gift of regeneration and renewal. His sacred evergreen holly, exchanged during the midwinter festival as a symbol of good luck, was believed to ward off lightning and evil spirits.

Farther north, the people of Scandinavia had their own magical gift bearer, the god Odin, who rode his eight-legged white steed, Sleipnir, across the sky delivering rewards and punishments. His son, Thor, the warrior god of thunder, traveled in his goat-drawn chariot, chasing away the cold and frost with thunderclaps and a lightning flash from his magic hammer.

As Christianity spread throughout Europe, Christians looked for an acceptable figure to replace the pagan gift bearers. They found one in the kindly saint and folk hero from Myra, St. Nicholas. Born in the third century to altruistic parents from rich and noble families, Nicholas was orphaned at a young age and raised by a loving uncle who taught him prayers and rituals. At nineteen he was ordained to the priesthood and at twenty-nine was appointed bishop of Myra, in ancient Lycia, today's Turkey. With the money

St. Nicholas, Bishop of Myra. Courtesy Dover Publications.

left to him by his father, Nicholas devoted his life to easing the suffering of the poor and needy.

Stories of Nicholas's kindness and miracles spread far and wide. He quelled tempests at sea and saved people from famine. He left food, money, and gifts at the windows of the needy. One story told of a penniless father with three daughters for whom he could not provide dowries and whom he was nearly forced to sell into slavery. But the daughters mysteriously received bags of gold coins, tossed down the chimney into stockings hung by the fire to dry. As a symbol of protection, Nicholas became the patron saint not only of children and childhood, but of orphans, sailors, maidens, and prisoners and of many lands, including Russia and Greece. On the eve of St. Nicholas Day, December 6, the day of his death, children left food for him and straw for his horse, and the next morning found them replaced by gifts.

With the Protestant Reformation and the banning of Catholic saints, St. Nicholas disappeared in most European countries, replaced by kindly gift bearers with nonreligious appearances. In Germany the spirit of generosity appeared as the angelic Christkindl, later known as Kris Kringle; in England as Father Christmas; in France as Père Noël; and in Italy as Bambino Natale. The figure of St. Nicholas survived in Holland, and when Dutch immigrants arrived in New Amsterdam (which would become New York) in the seventeenth century, they brought the tradition of St. Nicholas (*Sinterklass*) and the celebration of St. Nicholas Day.

The transformation of St. Nicholas—from a tall, dignified, bearded bishop in a glittering red robe on a fine white steed with gifts for good children and with his assistant, Black Peter, by his side with birch rods to punish bad children—to the jolly elf we now know began in 1809 with a satirical book by Washington Irving about Dutch customs in New York. Published under the pseudonym Diedrich Knickerbocker, *A History of New York from the Beginning of the World to the End of the Dutch Dynasty* described St. Nicholas as a jolly, pipe-smoking Dutchman who flew over treetops in a gift-filled wagon. One phrase in Irving's book, about St. Nicholas "laying his finger beside his nose," would appear a few years later in a poem by Clement Clarke Moore, a professor of divinity, whose poem *A Visit from St. Nicholas* would establish Santa Claus, a corruption of the Dutch *Sinterklaas,* as the embodiment of good cheer and generosity. A special edition of the poem, published in 1848 with engravings by Theodore C. Boyd, depicted Santa as a gnome-like

The evolution of Santa Claus. Courtesy Dover Publications.

character. It wasn't until the political cartoonist Thomas Nast, who was best known for his vitriolic attacks on corrupt politicians, began drawing evocative, enchanting Christmas scenes for *Harper's Weekly* in 1863 that Santa took on the image of an avuncular, fur-clad gent with a twinkle in his eye and a workshop at the North Pole.

By 1889 Santa had taken a wife. The Falmouth, Massachusetts–born poet and Wellesley College professor Katharine Lee Bates, best known as the author of "America, the Beautiful," wrote often about Christmas, a season that appealed to her childlike enthusiasm and wonder. In Bates's poem *Goody Santa Claus*, Mrs. Claus, the goodwife, made her first appearance:

> *Santa, must I tease in vain, Dear? Let me*
> *   go and hold the reindeer,*
> *While you clamber down the chimneys.*
> *   Don't look savage as a Turk!*
> *Why should you have all the glory of the*
> *   joyous Christmas story,*
> *And poor little Goody Santa Claus have*
> *   nothing but the work?*

Goody Santa Claus on a Sleigh-Ride, 1888.
Courtesy Wellesley College Archives.

There remained one last metamorphosis for Santa, which came in 1931 when the Coca-Cola Company commissioned a Chicago-based illustrator, Haddon Sundblom, to create a thoroughly American Santa Claus for an advertising campaign. Inspired by Moore's description of Santa in *A Visit from St. Nicholas,* Sundblom created the modern, larger-than-life icon of Santa.

(ABOVE LEFT) Santa listens to a child, 1968. Courtesy Boston Public Library Print Department.

(ABOVE) Santa with children at Jordan Marsh, 1960. Private collection.

(LEFT) Santa with children at Jordan Marsh, 1963. Private collection.

The Man Who Loved Christmas: James Van Alen

HE WAS BORN into privilege in 1902, in the gracious and courtly enclave of Newport, Rhode Island, and educated at Christ's College in Cambridge, England. If he is fondly remembered these days as a flamboyant socialite, James Van Alen is also remembered as a Renaissance man: a navy veteran of World War II, a published poet, an accomplished musician and songwriter, an ardent preservationist, and a nationally ranked tennis player. He contributed more to his beloved game of tennis than simply stellar play. It was James Van Alen ("Jimmy" to his friends) who developed a simplified scoring system that allowed a tie-breaker to determine the winner of sets. When the Newport Casino—an elegant private club and recreational facility built in the Victorian shingle style by McKim, Mead and White in 1879—was threatened with demolition in the early 1950s, Jimmy stepped in and saved the historic building. The Casino had been America's second court-tennis court, and Jimmy had learned to play lawn tennis at the club in 1915. He became the newly refurbished Casino's president in 1952 and in 1954 founded the International Tennis Hall of Fame on the site.

Van Alen was fun-loving and by all accounts a little bit mischievous, and his presence was never more keenly and joyously felt than it was during the Christmas season, when he gathered the children of Newport for his annual, dramatic reading of *A Visit from St. Nicholas*, better known as *'Twas the Night before Christmas,* written by a Newport summer resident, Clement C. Moore.

During a sleigh ride home on Christmas Eve in 1822 Moore, living in New York and teaching at the General Theological Seminary, dashed off the poem for his children, giving Santa—thought to be modeled on a jolly Dutchman who worked at the Moore home—a distinctly northern appearance as well as eight tiny reindeer, including Donder and Blitzen, whose names were Dutch for thunder and lightning. Moore, a respected scholar of Biblical and classical literature, never intended the poem for a wider audience or for publication, and he was said to have been deeply embarrassed when a family friend copied it into her journal and submitted it, without Moore's knowledge, to the *Troy Sentinel,* where it was published anonymously in December 1823.

Over the years, as the poem grew in popularity, the public clamored to know its author. Moore, thinking the fanciful story frivolous, was reluctant to accept credit for the poem until he finally acknowledged authorship in

1844—at the age of sixty-five—when he included it in a book of his poetry. Despite a lifetime of scholarship, Moore would be remembered for the magical poem—the most famous of all Christmas stories—that embodied the ideals of love and generosity. When he retired from teaching in the 1850s, he bought a rambling summer home on Catherine Street in Newport, and it was there that he died, just days before his eighty-fourth birthday, in July 1863.

James Van Alen had grown up fascinated by Moore's story of a mysterious, supernatural Christmas Eve visitor. In the early 1950s, a century after Moore had come to Newport, Van Alen began portraying him, dressed in elegant Victorian attire—with Mrs. Van Alen by his side, dressed as Mrs. Moore—reciting the poem to the wide-eyed children of Newport at Moore's Catherine Street home. Van Alen had dreamed of founding a Santa Claus Society and of preserving Moore's home as the Santa Claus House, complete with live reindeer, though the dream was never realized.

James Van Alen. Courtesy International Tennis Hall of Fame, Newport, Rhode Island.

The house, known as the Cedars or the Clement C. Moore House, still stands at 25 Catherine Street; there is a colorful tribute on its outside wall acknowledging Moore's timeless contribution to Christmas.

Van Alen's reading of *A Visit from St. Nicholas* became a beloved Newport tradition, the highlight of Newport's Christmas season, and Jimmy, who had long pondered what might have happened to the father—in his cap—after Santa had finished his work, finally took up his pen and added his own verses to the poem:

> *I leant far out listening,*
> *my hands on the sill*
> *No sound broke the silence,*
> *the night was so still,*
>
> *'Twas hard to believe just*
> *one moment before*

Saint Nick and his reindeer
had raced past my door.

The air clear as crystal was
frosty and crisp,
It turned the warm breath
from my lips to a whisp

Of cottony cloud just as
white and as thick
As the smoke from the short
stumpy pipe of Saint Nick.

Van Alen's readings continued for nearly forty years, until his untimely death from a fall in 1991. If Clement C. Moore has brought joy to countless children, so too had James Van Alen, whose twinkling eyes and merry smile warmed the coldest of Newport nights. Despite his life of privilege amid the grandeur of Ocean Avenue, Jimmy Van Alen always knew that it is the simple joys of the season that are best remembered and that the gift of oneself, especially when shared with children, is the best gift of all.

Silent Santa

IMAGINE BEING A child, seven or eight years old, who has never had the chance to sit with Santa and go over that special Christmas list. No chance to ask for a doll or truck or, as is sometimes the case, to convey to Santa a heartfelt wish for a struggling mom or dad, or a sick brother or sister.

For countless children who are deaf or hearing impaired, there's never been and may never be a visit with Santa. They can only stand in the background, in their own silent world, and watch as hearing children, sometimes their own brothers and sisters, climb aboard Santa's knee and experience that joyful rite of childhood.

But there is a place—Carl Bozenski's Christmas Village in Torrington, Connecticut—where hearing-impaired children have their own special "Silent Santa." There they "talk" to Santa and experience the magic that most hearing children, and their parents, take for granted.

When he takes his big, red suit off, Santa is Bob Smith, a translator for the State Commission on the Deaf and Hearing Impaired. Back in the early

Bob Smith, the Silent Santa, signing "I love you." Photo by Tom Kabelka,
courtesy *Republican-American*, Waterbury, Connecticut.

1980s, when he first donned the suit and tucked in a soft pillow to better
play the part (when he needs new glasses he tells his optometrist they must
be "Santa" glasses), Bob never imagined the joy that he could bring, so simply, to deaf children—or the depth of the pure, childlike joy that they
would evoke in him.

It all began at Northwestern Connecticut Community College in Winsted
when Bob, a business major, signed up for an American Sign Language elec-
tive course. Connecticut had always been at the forefront in providing services for the hearing impaired. The college, not far from West Hartford's
American School for the Deaf, the first school for the deaf in America, had
always been popular with hearing-impaired students.

Bob found that he had an aptitude for ASL and promptly changed his
major. Living with two deaf roommates helped his fluency, and a conversa-
tion with a representative from the State Commission who had come to the
school to give a lecture led to Bob being offered a job as a translator. It was,
he says happily, fate.

Not long after he started work with the commission, the town of Madison contacted the office and asked if there might be someone who could play Silent Santa for a deaf child who would be attending the annual Christmas parade. So heartwarming was the experience of being able to give the young child his first meeting with Santa that Bob offered to play Santa wherever he might be needed. His future as Santa would be sealed a year later at a mall in Milford.

A mother and her child, a seven-year-old deaf girl, approached him, and Bob could see the child's distress. Unbeknown to the little girl, Santa was "listening" to everything she was saying to her mother.

"Why are you making me do this?" she signed frantically to her mother. "I can't talk to Santa. I'm deaf." Mom, who knew that Bob was Silent Santa and had prearranged the visit, begged the child to visit Santa. The little girl continued to protest and then the tears began to flow. She glanced Santa's way, and when she caught Bob's eye he signed to her, "Would you like to visit with Santa?" Bob says it was a moment he will never forget, and he still gets emotional remembering it years later. Her eyes lit up and sparkled. She ran toward him and leaped into his lap. Bob says he knew at that moment that he would always be Silent Santa.

Since the early 1990s Bob, who now works (when he's not at the North Pole) for the Torrington Area Health District, has volunteered one evening each December to play Silent Santa at Torrington's annual, monthlong Christmas Village. The village began in 1947, when Carl Bozenski, then a supervisor for recreation for the City of Torrington, had the storybook idea to recreate Santa's North Pole for the children of Torrington. Alvord Playground and its small park proved to be the perfect setting for Santa's parlor, his workshop, and his team of eight reindeer. For Bob Smith, the evening at the village is the highlight of his Christmas season. Advertised well in advance, Bob's silent presence draws families from Connecticut, Rhode Island, and Massachusetts. He sees hearing kids with deaf parents, deaf kids with hearing parents, and children with disabilities that require them to communicate by sign language. For most it will be their first visit with Santa, and Bob makes the most of the experience, spending extra time with them, making up for all their lost visits.

Ask Bob, who on those special evenings also plays Santa to hearing kids, if he has seen any difference over the years in the Christmas lists, in the way deaf children approach Santa, in the way they express their hopes and dreams, and he'll tell you emphatically: no. Hearing-impaired kids are no different from any other kids.

We are all Santa's children, and therein may be the best lesson of the season.

Flying Santa

ONLY ONE AMERICAN lighthouse still feels a human presence. In the 1980s, in a move to cut costs, the Coast Guard, responsible for lighthouses since 1939, automated every light except Boston Light, the nation's oldest lighthouse site. Lighthouse keepers and their families were brought ashore and a heroic way of life—what the New England historian Edward Rowe Snow called a "story of romance, adventure, loneliness and danger"—passed into history.

Flying Santa, Edward Rowe Snow, and his family.
Courtesy Dolly Snow Bicknell.

We have received your package.
We thank you kindly for including us on your list, and
you may rest assured that the contents of your Christmas
parcel spread joy to the personnel attached to this unit.
"A Pilgrim Returns to Cape Cod" has been read by several
of the fellows previously, and we hope that the remaining
"strangers" will enjoy it fully as much as we did. A
happy and joyous Christmas to you and yours, followed by
a full year of health and prosperity.

Roy Scott, BM(L)
Nauset Lifeboat Station
U. S. Coast Guard
Eastham, Massachusetts

THE FLYING SANTA   EDWARD ROWE SNOW
SUMMER STREET
MARSHFIELD, MASS.

We have received the package
Thanks from   SCHOOL AT CLIFF
Roberta MacVane   Kelly J O'Reilly
Ann MacVane   Andrea Meyerowitz
Brian O'Reilly   JAN
Robert MacVane
David MacVane III   (Benjie + Dawn)
Nanette Dyer   absent
Merry Christmas!   Laurie MacVane
Sandra Meyerowitz
(Teacher at the Cliff Island School)

Flying Santa postcards, c. 1957.
Courtesy Dolly Snow Bicknell.

As modern technology continues to provide mariners with sophisticated navigational systems and computerized charts, it becomes harder and harder to remember a time when the light from an oil lamp and the drone from a foghorn inspired hope—and saved lives. And as modern technology finds new ways to connect people to one another and to shrink the world, it becomes harder, too, to imagine the isolation that lighthouse keepers and their families experienced living alone on tiny, far-flung, storm-buffeted, fog-enshrouded rocks, islands, and ledges.

No time of the year was lonelier than December as winter set in: the winds began to howl and, all over New England and America, families and friends were gathering to share in the spirit of Christmas. But for lighthouse keepers and their families, there was no Christmas, no respite from duties and responsibilities. Christmas was a day like any other, until 1929, when a seaplane pilot named Bill Wincapaw brought Christmas to the lighthouses.

Captain Bill Wincapaw, a native of Friendship, Maine, had become a lifeline for the islanders of Penobscot Bay. Delivering mail and supplies and transporting the sick and injured to the mainland for treatment, he was well known to the lighthouse families who had become *his* lifeline. They watched for his plane and radioed ahead to alert the next post to his approach. Through the darkest of nights and the worst of weather they guided him safely home.

On pleasant summer days, Wincapaw often landed his seaplane and visited with keepers and their families. He understood their isolation, their craving for human fellowship, the awesome responsibility they had to mariners and pilots. His considered them the *true* lifesavers, and, to show his appreciation, he loaded his seaplane with wrapped Christmas presents in December 1929 and retraced his regular route, dropping gifts from his plane at the lonely outposts.

His gesture, he thought, was small, his gifts mere tokens. The packages contained modest, useful items—magazines and newspapers, coffee and candy—but for families accustomed to making do with little, they were luxuries. And for many families, it was the first opportunity in years to "celebrate" Christmas.

Word got back to the "Flying Santa" that his gesture of goodwill had been well received, that families appreciated being remembered. So the following year the Christmas flight was repeated, and over the next few years it expanded into Massachusetts, Rhode Island, and Connecticut. Captain Wincapaw began dressing as Santa and was joined on the flights by his teenage son, Bill Jr., an aspiring pilot. Sponsors stepped forward to assist with the purchase of gifts, which were dropped at nearly one hundred lighthouses and Coast Guard lifesaving stations up and down the New England coast.

The Wincapaw family's move from Maine to Winthrop, Massachusetts, proved fortuitous. Young Bill introduced his father to one of his teachers at Winthrop High School, the dashing Edward Rowe Snow, who, though only in his early thirties, had already lived a lifetime of adventure. Snow had a keen interest in the lore and legends of the New England coast, including the mysteries and tragedies surrounding lighthouses. In 1935 he published the first of his ninety-seven books, *The Islands of Boston Harbor,* and the following year was invited to join the Wincapaws on their Christmas flights. By 1947 Snow had made the role of Flying Santa his own; he expanded deliveries to Bermuda, Newfoundland, Labrador, and the Pacific Coast. He continued his flights for the next thirty-five years, until his death in 1982.

Every December, on the Snow family Ping-Pong table that served as a staging area, gifts were wrapped by Flying Santa and his elves—his devoted wife, Anna-Myrle, and later his daughter, Dolly—in newspaper and excelsior. Marked with a letter to identify the family member the package was intended for—there was even a "D" for dog—the packages included pens and pencils, balls and dolls, books, sunglasses, cigars and cigarettes, balloons and chewing gum. Snow also included a copy of his latest book and a self-addressed, stamped postcard with the message "We have received your package" typed or handwritten. On the basis of the returned postcards, Snow boasted that 94 percent of the packages he dropped were successfully delivered.

There was, however, the occasional "miss," such as the package that landed in the water some forty feet from Whaleback Light in Portsmouth Harbor. Snow called it "one of my more outstanding failures," and he promptly dropped a second package—right on target. But the story didn't end there. The errant package floated ninety miles to Sandwich, Massachusetts, where it was picked up. The soggy, self-addressed, stamped postcard was returned to Snow.

But for every miss and disappointment, there were a hundred stories of sheer joy as Santa's love rained down from the sky. And no story was more heartwarming than the story of little Seamond Ponsart. It was December 1945 and the Ponsart family was stationed on Cuttyhunk Island, on the remote edge of the Elizabeth Islands in Massachusetts. Seamond eagerly awaited the arrival of Flying Santa, who, she knew, was bringing a special doll. The day finally arrived and, right on schedule, Santa's plane appeared overhead; packages tumbled out the window. Santa waved good-bye and the Ponsart family and coast guardsmen scrambled in the bitter cold to gather up the bundles.

In the warmth of the keeper's house, one by one the packages were opened until, finally, the last package was unwrapped. It was Seamond's beautiful doll, but it had been dashed to pieces by the fall. Seamond went to bed that night heartbroken. Her mother returned Santa's postcard, thanking him for his kindness and for the doll, but explaining that the doll had been broken on the rocks. Santa was equally distressed: of all his gifts, it was the special doll that had been broken.

Santa did not forget Seamond. The next year, after their beloved Cutty-hunk Light was condemned, the Ponsart family was transferred to West Chop Light on Martha's Vineyard. Flying Santa contacted the Ponsarts and asked them to take Seamond on a particular day to the lifesaving station at Gay Head. As Seamond waited, not knowing why she was there, Santa magically appeared in a helicopter chartered at his own expense for the special visit. He personally presented six-year-old Seamond with a new doll.

Over the years the Ponsart family stayed in touch with Flying Santa, and after his death they corresponded with Mrs. Santa, Anna-Myrle Snow. In 2000, a memorial was dedicated to Edward Rowe Snow on Georges Island in Boston Harbor. Seamond Ponsart, the lighthouse keeper's daughter whose childhood friends had been her dogs, cats, and chickens, was then a Coast Guard officer in New Orleans. She had never forgotten the fairy-tale visit by Flying Santa, and, though unable to attend the ceremony, she wrote a letter that was read at the dedication. Her beloved Flying Santa had long since passed away, but Seamond remembered that meeting him, this "hero of mine," was the "pinnacle event" of her life. "He knew this would make me happy and he did it because he was a big-hearted man and knew the real

Hello Santa: leaving Flying Santa a Christmas message, c. 1948.
Courtesy Monhegan Historical and Cultural Museum Organization.

A Lighthouse Keeper's Christmas Memories

To you landsmen and women a snowy Christmas generally means the day is complete; but to the lighthouse keeper it is too often ushered in by a northeast gale. As far as the eye can reach under the light I see nothing but the fast-driving flakes, while the sea dashes white on the rocks and is a visitor at my windows, knocking noisily every few minutes. The wind shrieks through the old house, rushes through the lantern with a noise like the shrill whistle of a steamboat foretelling danger, and even round the doors there is a chorus as if an army of fiends were attacking us. But with all this against us in the elements, in my girlish days we had many jolly Christmases, for we were a large family of boys and girls and liked, just as I do today, the pleasant giving and receiving of gifts, which marks the birthday of Christ. Now, with only my brother Rudolph left, we make the day as jovial as can be, and my dinner, with its turkey and "fixings" of celery and cranberry sauce, its mince pies and plum pudding, I should like to share with you all. And with the good things of the day, the dinner and the gifts, goes my Christmas wish to each and all, the same as that of Tiny Tim. "God bless us, every one."

—Ida Lewis, Keeper, Lime Rock Light, Newport, Rhode Island, 1890

meaning of reaching out to people," wrote Seamond. "I felt like I had been crowned queen forever."

In 2003 Seamond had the opportunity to be a guest elf on a Flying Santa flight sponsored by the Friends of Flying Santa, the nonprofit organization founded in 1997 to ensure the continuation of the Christmas flights. She was delighted to revisit her cherished childhood memories and finally meet Flying Santa's daughter, Dolly.

If ever there was a flesh-and-blood Santa who came close to the magical being of childhood, it was Edward Rowe Snow, who came and went out of thin air, "delivering love from an airplane." With his robust physique, shock of white hair, gentle nature, and good cheer, he seemed born to be Santa. Why, his very name evoked the Christmas spirit!

For thousands of children like Seamond Ponsart, Edward Rowe Snow was kindness and love personified. He had, she said, the ability to make each child feel so special that they all referred to him as "my Flying Santa."

Two Santas for Boston

BENEATH THE VENEER of society's prosperity there is an enormous need, not for the luxuries in life, not even for the simple pleasures in life, but for the basic, bare necessities. For too many children the floor beneath the Christmas tree (if there is a tree) is cold and empty on Christmas morning. For parents and grandparents who find it a daily, desperate struggle simply to feed and clothe children, to keep them warm and safe, Christmas is anything but a time for celebration, joy, and gift giving. It is, rather, often just another bleak day, one of the many that have defined the year.

But for children, even those whose circumstances are dire, Christmas is always a magical day, a day with a mysterious power to bring joy and to bring people together. In their innocence, children have faith that Santa Claus will not pass them by; with the help of two Santas, Globe Santa and Secret Santa, many of Boston's neediest children will, indeed, have a merry Christmas.

When the *Boston Globe* Newspaper Company bought the venerable old *Boston Post* back in the mid-1950s, it acquired not only the *Post*'s readers, but also its well-established Christmas appeal for the needy begun by Edwin Grozier, a philanthropist and the *Post*'s owner. In 1956 Globe Santa debuted and, every year since, this modern-day incarnation of the true meaning of Christmas has helped needy families in the Greater Boston area share in the joy of the season.

Preparations begin even before retailers start bedecking their stores, when social service and religious agencies—more than two hundred welfare offices, hospitals, churches, clergy, and halfway houses—register with the Globe Santa Fund. During October and November, families apply for assistance, specifying their family size and need. All letters must be verified and countersigned by registered agencies.

Globe staffers, sequestered in a basement office at the paper's Morrissey Boulevard headquarters, meticulously sort through the avalanche of mail, reading and verifying every letter sent to Globe Santa. Meanwhile, generous *Globe* readers and advertisers, businesses, social clubs, restaurants, and schools—people who know that they have the power to work a miracle for a child—spring into action, donating money, more than $1 million each year for the last twenty years, every penny of which is used for the purchase of gifts. Kids from all over the Boston area send their paper route money and babysitting money. Many who donate were themselves helped at one time by Globe Santa; now they have the chance to return the kindness.

The name of every donor is published in the paper along with a daily tally of the money raised. The *Globe* ownership generously assumes all the administrative costs of the program—verifying the letters, counting donations, packing toys—and each day the paper features a story of a needy family's circumstances. Heartbreaking and desperate though the stories may be, these families, at least for a day, will experience the uplifting joy of the season and the blessings of the community.

Working with a toy broker, Santa's elves purchase quality toys, books, and stuffed animals. Beginning the first week in December and continuing until two days before Christmas, presents are mailed to families. More than 59,000 children from 29,000 families are visited by Globe Santa each year; he distributes 30,000 stuffed animals, 60,000 books, and 90,000 toys. To ensure all deliveries, and to guarantee that no child is disappointed on Christmas morning, a signature is required for all packages.

Meanwhile, at Boston's General Mail Facility, which serves more than one hundred post offices in the Greater Boston area, postal employees handle more than 10,000 letters to Santa each Christmas season. Many are snazzy, computer-generated wish lists that will be answered by a pleasant form letter from Santa expressing his hope that the writer has been a good little boy or girl all year. But more than 3,000 letters will be heartbreaking requests from moms and dads asking for help for their kids.

If the words of those letters are not sorrow-filled enough, consider the mother or father who, having long ago given up on a flesh-and-blood Santa, takes up pen and paper and writes to Santa Claus, c/o North Pole, asking for a pair of sneakers, a warm jacket, a pair of mittens, anything so that there will be something under the tree on Christmas morning.

Occasionally, older children write, asking for nothing for themselves but for a stuffed animal for a baby sister, a truck for a baby brother, an operation for a sick mother, a job for an out-of-work father. A letter to Santa from an adult, despondent at the thought of having failed a child, seems an act of quiet desperation, a last hope, but at Boston's General Mail Facility Santa's helpers, in the disguise of unheralded postal workers, will make certain that

Christmas mail, 1959. Courtesy Boston Public Library Print Department.

for this one day at least, all children in need will have something to brighten their day.

No one knows for sure when the Secret Santa program at the post office began—at least thirty-five years ago—but it has become one of Boston's quiet Christmas traditions. Postal employees, for whom Secret Santa is a much-anticipated labor of love, sort the piles of letters, all of which must be certified by a social services agency or clergyman. Letters are then made available to a network of Santa's helpers who "adopt" a family and work with that family to shop, wrap, and deliver gifts. Like Globe Santa, Secret Santa operates on the simple premises that no child should go without a present on Christmas Day, and that we all should endeavor to keep the illusion of Santa alive for children as long as we can. Reality, as most grownups know, comes all too soon enough.

Globe Santa Letter

Dear Santa:

We are writing to you in hopes that you can make our Christmas a happy one. Last year our Mom left. She's out of our life but her heart is with us. Our Grandma has custody of us. Our wish is that our family will all be together. I know it's a lot to ask, but Santa and God will hear you.

Our Grandma works very hard. She takes care of us, pays the bills, cleans the house, and so much more. Without money for toys, we hope Globe Santa can come to our house and help Grandma out. My name is Doreen. I'm 6 years old and all I want is a beautiful doll. My brother's name is Robert. He's 8 and likes games. But whatever you can send us will be greatly appreciated. We also love books to read. Grandma reads us books all the time.

Well, I need to go now, so I'll be good and I hope I see you at Christmas.

Love to you,

Doreen

—Courtesy *Boston Globe.*

Rudolph, the Most Famous Reindeer

IN THE SUMMER of 1939, as retailers began to plan for the approaching Christmas season, there was little to suggest that happier days were ahead. The world, already suffering through the decadelong Depression, was then on the brink of war. One company, the Chicago-based Montgomery Ward, hoped to lift spirits— and profits—with a special giveaway, a Christmas storybook. For years the giant catalog company, like other retailers, had distributed a Christmas coloring book to children, but in 1939 company managers envisioned something new and different that would set them apart from the competition. For ideas and inspiration they turned to a young, soft-spoken but clever copywriter, Robert May.

May, then thirty-four years old and the father of four-year-old Barbara, was suffering through his own dark days. Whatever promise there might have been in the years after his graduation from Dartmouth College in 1926 had not yet been realized. For a paltry salary he spent his days turning out ad copy for Montgomery Ward's mail order catalog. His young wife was dying and her mounting medical bills had plunged the family deep into debt. He was unable to explain the pervasive sadness to little Barbara, who asked why her mommy wasn't like everyone else's.

Little around him seemed to promise hope, but during the summer of 1939, May immersed himself in his new project. He needed a main character for his Christmas story, and he remembered the joy Barbara always took when she visited the reindeer at the local zoo. But what, he wondered, could another reindeer accomplish that Dasher, Dancer, Prancer, Vixen, Comet, Cupid, Donder, and Blitzen weren't already handily taking care of?

May thought about his childhood as a small and delicate boy who had often been taunted by schoolmates. He had gone to Dartmouth in the early 1920s, when the school, founded in 1769 on what had been the frontier of European settlement, was still an all-male college with an outdoors, wilderness state of mind. He understood what it was like to be discriminated against, to be an outsider, and he drew on those feelings in shaping his storybook character.

After considering a number of names for his reindeer—Rollo and Reginald among them—he settled on Rudolph, and decided that Rudolph would have something the other reindeer didn't have:

> *Where most reindeers' noses are brownish and tiny,*
> *Poor Rudolph's was red, very large, and quite shiny.*

May's bosses at Montgomery Ward were reluctant to embrace the story of a lonesome reindeer with a red nose and worried that the nose might be associated with inebriation. But May, convinced that his Rudolph was the perfect character around whom to tell his story, secretly went to his friend in the art department, Denver Gillen, and asked him to draw a cute, lovable reindeer with a big, red nose.

With drawings in hand, May met again with his bosses, who saw the potential in Rudolph. May got busy finishing his story, *The Day before Christmas* or *Rudolph, the Red-Nosed Reindeer,* writing 178 lines in 89 rhyming couplets that echoed one of his favorite poems, *A Visit from St. Nicholas.*

May's book—an instant hit for Montgomery Ward and a timely message of hope for Americans—told the story of an underdog reindeer who, though ostracized by the reindeer community, knew he had been a good little reindeer and went to bed on Christmas Eve hopeful that Santa wouldn't pass him by. Sleeping soundly, his nose glowing in the dark, he was discovered by Santa, quite by accident, and asked to lead the other reindeer through the fog and dark. Two and a half million copies of the book were distributed the first year, and though wartime shortages limited printing over the next several years, by 1946 more than six million books were in print. Requests for Rudolph merchandise poured in.

Montgomery Ward held the copyright on Rudolph until 1947, but that Christmas May's bosses presented it to him as a Christmas gift. The copyright gave May, who remarried and fathered five more children, the financial success that had for so long eluded him. Rudolph's story was reissued by a commercial publisher and in 1949 was set to music by May's brother-in-law, the popular songwriter Johnny Marks. Recorded by Gene Autry, the song made Rudolph the "most famous reindeer of all" and inspired a 1964 animated film, narrated by Burl Ives, which has since become a perennial Christmas favorite.

In 1958 Robert May donated his papers to Dartmouth College in New Hampshire, where, in a small red folio, the original layout for Rudolph has been lovingly conserved. Its thirty-two illustrated pages—tracing paper adhered to manila card stock with rubber cement—show May's editorial instructions for Rudolph's "green tears" and his excitement ("Eager for the job—bounding out!") as he took his place at the head of the sleigh. May's original manuscript, written in pencil in longhand on a legal pad, with all the underlines, erasures, "stets," and "moves" that ultimately made the story what it is, offers a fascinating insight into the creative process.

Born of a dark time in our nation's history and in Robert May's personal history, Rudolph and his message are just as inspirational today: Believe in yourself. Brighter days are always ahead. And we all have our own special gift awaiting our own special Santa to set it free.

A Magical Ride on the Polar Express

DURING DECEMBER a train makes its way slowly through the dark and quiet of New Hampshire's White Mountains. This, though, is no ordinary train, but one that twinkles with

Christmas lights and whose passengers are wide-eyed children dressed in pajamas and nightgowns on their way to the North Pole. For two hours they will live the magical, otherworldly experience of the little boy in Chris Van Allsburg's classic Christmas story, *The Polar Express.*

If ever there was an antidote for the cynicism and commercialism of Christmas, it is the Polar Express event, a cherished Christmas tradition created and sponsored by the New Hampshire–based Believe in Books Literacy Foundation. The train ride, which delights some twenty thousand children and adults each Christmas season, grew out of a desire a decade ago to create a small event that would spark both community spirit during the Christmas season and an appreciation of reading and literature.

Event organizers looked for their inspiration to Van Allsburg's timeless and ageless book, published in 1985. A recipient of the prestigious Caldecott Medal, *The Polar Express* is the enchanting story of a young boy—told by his friends that there is no Santa Claus—whose faith takes him on a magical Christmas Eve train ride to the North Pole. There not only does he meet Santa at his toy- and elf-filled workshop, but he is chosen by Santa to receive the very first gift of Christmas. Though he could have any gift from Santa's workshop, the boy asks only for a bell from the reindeers' harness.

Back on the train, bound for home, the boy discovers that the bell he thought was safely tucked in his bathrobe pocket has been lost. Heartbroken, he arrives home and waves good-bye to the conductor, only to find on Christmas morning that his silver bell is wrapped in a small box under the tree. The boy and his sister can hear the bell's ring, but his parents cannot. In time, his sister can no longer hear the bell's sweet sound, but he, through the transforming power of faith, still hears the bell even when he has grown old.

At the heart of *The Polar Express*—and the heart of the Christmas season—is faith. Since ancient times the season has been about faith, faith that the life-giving sun would return, faith that the Son would come to save mankind. Bells, believed since ancient times to possess magical powers, were used to chase away the dark of midwinter. Later they were symbolic of the communion between God and man, the clappers said to be the tongues of angels.

As a "living performance," different from other Polar Express and Santa Express train rides, the Polar Express event stays true to the book. Trains, contracted from the Conway Scenic Railroad in North Conway and the

Hobo Railroad in Lincoln, roll over peaks and through valleys, through the "quiet wilderness." Passengers are served "cocoa as thick and rich as melted chocolate bars" and "candies with nougat centers as white as snow." As trains pull in at the North Pole depot, passengers are met by Santa's elves and then escorted by lantern light to a cozy theater in the half-round. The little boy of the story, now grown old, comes onstage to read his story. Van Allsburg's evocative, shadowy, pastel illustrations are projected in the theater during the storytelling, after which Santa visits with the children and chooses one to receive the bell from the reindeers' harness. But, in the event's one departure from the book, the boy is given a second wish—that all the children receive a silver bell.

Proceeds from the first Polar Express event were donated to various literacy organizations, but by the late 1990s the success of the event had spawned the nonprofit Believe in Books Literacy Foundation, whose founders believed that too many people are excluded from the joys of reading because they don't have basic skills or books. Today more than a thousand volunteers from the North Conway area—committed not only to the heavenly goal of making Christmas magical, but also to the earthly goal of sharing books and reading—give their time and energies to the Polar Express event. On any given night, several hundred "elves" ride the trains and fill the workshop, delighting children and, through that transforming power of faith, giving grownups the chance to hear the bell's sweet sound once again.

IV. Gifts and Greetings

A T THE HEART of the ancient Roman Saturnalia festival was the exchange of gifts, called *strenae,* and greetings of goodwill. Given out of a desire to share one's abundance, gifts were traditionally exchanged on the Kalends of January, New Year's Day, in honor of Father Time and the god Janus. At first the offerings were small, with symbolic meaning. Twigs and boughs from the sacred grove of Strenia, the woodland goddess, were given as expressions of good luck and bounty for the coming year. Wax tapers promised to light one's journey through life. Gold coins prophesied prosperity; sweets, sugared cakes, and honey foretold happiness.

In time, gift giving became more extravagant. In his book *Christmas Customs and Traditions,* Clement Miles relates an account by the fourth-century Greek scholar and teacher of rhetoric Libanius, who wrote that during the Kalends the "impulse to spend seizes everyone. He who the whole year through has taken pleasure in saving and piling up his pence, becomes suddenly extravagant. . . . People are not only generous toward themselves, but

Get this Christmas present to-day

Courtesy Dover Publications.

57

also toward their fellow-man. A stream of presents pours itself out on all sides."

Though early Christians frowned on the practice of gift giving, many were reluctant to part with the custom. The Roman Church found justification in the practice of gift giving in the Divine Child and his ultimate gift of himself, and in the story of the Magi and their symbolic gifts of gold, frankincense, and myrrh. By the Middle Ages, Christmas itself had become all too pagan, an extravagant public display of conspicuous consumption

Courtesy Dover Publications.

and impulsive spending. The Protestant Reformation and Puritanism put the brakes on Christmas excess, though both movements approved of small tokens of friendship exchanged for the New Year. By the time the holiday began its renaissance in England in the early nineteenth century, it had become a quiet day of rest and spiritual reflection spent in church and at home with family and friends. Simple, homemade gifts of peanut brittle, jams, bookmarks, pomander balls, and needlepoint were exchanged among grownups. Children, so as to not be spoiled, received one or two small presents: perhaps an orange or a pair of handmade mittens.

In 1843 the publication of Charles Dickens's *A Christmas Carol*, with its intimate family scenes and revelry, helped to further revive the holiday. The book's most powerful effect, however, was in awakening people to the plight of the needy among them, inspiring those with the means to undertake charitable giving. Money was pledged, gift boxes delivered, and dinners served. Charity became and would remain an integral part of Christmas giving.

By the middle and later Victorian years, years of opulence and extravagance, the "virtues" of gift giving were celebrated by the royal family, who lavished the royal children with toys and candies. The royal family captured the public's imagination and set the perfect example of how Christmas might be celebrated. Their subjects, eager to emulate the queen and her prince, Albert, turned gift giving into no small part of the season. The "stream of presents" that poured itself out happened to coincide with the new industrialization and a burgeoning middle class with money to spend on mass-produced, affordable merchandise.

The same year that Dickens penned his "Little Carol," as he called it, Sir Henry Cole, the civil servant and art patron who founded London's Victoria and Albert Museum, commissioned John Calcott Horsley, a member of the Royal Academy, to design a Christmas greeting, the Christmas card. Greeting cards were not new; predating the Christmas card by more than fifty years were New Year's greetings sent by merchants to their customers. But a special card at Christmas *was* new and though instantly popular in England, it would be another three decades before a German immigrant named Louis Prang would begin the tradition in New England.

Louis Prang, Father of the American Christmas Card

AMERICANS send more than two billion Christmas cards each year, and each American family, on average, sends and receives some thirty Christmas cards or letters. We can thank an enterprising German chromolithographer named Louis Prang, who set up shop in Boston, for the seasonal lift to our spirits and the welcome respite, however brief, from the daily onslaught of junk mail.

Born in 1824 in Breslau, Germany, Prang first learned color mixing and engraving techniques while apprenticing in his father's cloth factory. In his mid-twenties and caught up in the student revolutionary movement that swept Europe, Prang found himself on the wrong side of the 1848 Revolu-

(LEFT) Louis Prang. Courtesy Hallmark Archives, Hallmark Cards, Inc.

(RIGHT) L. Prang and Company, Boston, c. 1865. Courtesy Hallmark Archives, Hallmark Cards, Inc.

tion. Forced to flee his native Germany, he traveled first to Switzerland, then to New York, and by 1850 he had settled in Boston. Filled with hope and entrepreneurial spirit, he worked as an engraver for *Gleason's Pictorial* and in 1856 formed a partnership with another German American, Julius Mayer.

It wasn't long before the business-savvy Prang had struck out on his own. With a eye for what popular taste craved, Prang found success printing Civil War–related campaign maps, sheet music covers, and lithographic portraits of Union soldiers; by 1864 his firm, L. Prang and Company, was flourishing. Eager to nurture art appreciation and bring quality art—then available only to the well-to-do—into middle-class homes, he traveled to Europe to learn more about a new printing process called chromolithography.

Back in Boston, Prang perfected the chromolithographic process and began accurately reproducing full-size oil paintings by European masters. Where earlier coloring techniques used a one- or two-color printing process or were simply hand-tinted black and white illustrations, Prang's "chromos" were printed using a series of zinc plates—one plate for each color—and as many as thirty colors. Through detailed outlining, shading, and layering, he achieved a richness and complexity of design and hue never before seen in color reproduction. Varnished to look like real oil paintings and mounted in ornate frames, the pictures proved to be wildly popular with a wide audience. Prang was not without his detractors, however, who argued that his "art" was mere imitation. The critics, however, had little effect on collectors, who couldn't get enough of Prang's masterful color.

A new opportunity presented itself to Prang in 1873. Exhibiting his chromos, including business and greeting cards, at the Vienna Exposition, he was approached by the wife of his London agent. She had seen Christmas cards, already introduced in England, and suggested that Prang add a simple holiday sentiment to the scroll area on his business and greeting cards. Though America had only recently embraced Christmas as a holiday, Prang liked the idea. Using the floral and landscape designs from his business and greeting cards—not the iconography generally associated with Christmas— Prang published a selection of Christmas cards. He exported them to England that first year, so it wasn't until the following year that Americans had an opportunity to buy and send a Prang Christmas card. By 1877 an expanding railroad network and uniform postal rates made Prang cards available throughout the country.

That same year a devastating fire nearly destroyed the factory Prang had built a decade earlier. The *Boston Evening Transcript* for Thursday, September 27, 1877, reported: "Soon after four o'clock this morning, a lamplighter, while passing by the establishment of Louis Prang & Co., situated at the corner of Roxbury and Gardner Streets at the Highlands, discovered that the building was on fire. . . . The fire spread rapidly, and the entire building was soon in flames. . . . How great the loss was cannot be estimated, but it was very heavy, probably between $75,000 and $80,000."

But Prang was not discouraged. He moved to temporary quarters while repairs were made to his factory, and by March 1878 he was back at his old address.

The fanciest of Prang's cards, opulently decorated with touches of Victorian lace, velvet, and tassels, were essentially Christmas "valentines." Costing as much as twenty-five dollars, they were in themselves works of art and were often framed and given as gifts. A unique feature of the Prang card was the verse on the back of the card, written by well-known poets of the day, such as Henry Wadsworth Longfellow, John Greenleaf Whittier, and Celia Thaxter, whose sentiments in 1881 were typical of the time:

> *Christmas Look with smiles into thy face,*
> *Bring thee greetings glad, and gifts of grace,*
> *Scatter wishes kind about thy way,*
> *Thick as buds upon the boughs, in May.*
>
> *New Year steals upon the wintry shore;*
> *May she lead good fortune to thy door!*
> *Love and honor hasten thee to meet,*
> *Beauty clothe thy life with blossoms sweet!*

By 1880, eager for new, high-quality designs, Prang introduced the first of four annual design competitions judged by such art notables as John La Farge and Stanford White. With prize money totaling $2,000—the first prize was a then phenomenal $1,000—the competition attracted eight hundred entries. The following year, more than fifteen hundred entries were received. Prang's competitions not only generated fresh designs, but nurtured and encouraged art expression by American students, particularly women, something on which Prang would increasingly focus his energy.

Prang cards dominated the Christmas and greeting card market during the 1880s, and the Roxbury factory—which provided respectable employment for women—published more than five million cards annually. By

1890, however, inexpensive and inferior cards, imported from Germany, had flooded the market, and Louis Prang, rather than compromise quality, chose to abandon the Christmas card business altogether. He spent the next two decades promoting art education, authoring numerous art textbooks, and developing art materials, including his famous color wheel. Having already earned recognition as the "Father of the American Christmas card," Prang added another honor, "Father of Art Education in America."

Each year the greeting card industry awards its LOUIE Award for creative excellence in card design. In 1974 Louis Prang was honored by the U.S. Postal Service, the same postal service that ensured prompt delivery of his elegant cards a century earlier, with a commemorative stamp.

As for Boston, though Prang and his factory are gone, Prang is not forgotten. Thousands of his exquisite Christmas cards and chromos stayed in Boston and are now cared for, as carefully as they were by their first recipients, by the Print Department of the Boston Public Library.

Christmas in the City: Some Miracles Are Divine, Others Human

ON A CHRISTMAS morning in the late 1980s, Jake and Sparky Kennedy took one look at the avalanche of presents under the tree for their two young children, who wanted for nothing. In their own words, they were horrified by the extravagance. Determined not to repeat the indulgence the next year, Jake and Sparky limited their gifts to three per child, but found they were powerless to stem the flow of gifts from well-intentioned aunts, uncles, and grandparents. It wasn't just the overindulgence of their own children that distressed the Kennedys; they knew how many other children were awakening Christmas morning to nothing under the tree, if there was a tree at all.

How, Jake and Sparky wondered, could the true spirit of Christmas be rekindled? How could they begin to teach their children that Christmas was more than a pile of gifts? How could the family share some of its own good fortune with the less fortunate? The next year the Kennedys enlisted family and friends and organized a party in the lobby of Boston City Hall for 165 youngsters living in Boston-area shelters. Each child who attended the party had the chance to visit with Santa and was given a gift from his or her "wish list." The gifts had been purchased with donations collected in a glass jar at Jake Kennedy's physical therapy practice in downtown Boston. The communal celebration was capped with a holiday meal. Little did anyone, including

New England Christmas Home Scenes, and Christmas Games.
From *Ballou's Pictorial Drawingroom Companion,* 1853. Courtesy Dover Publications.

the Kennedys, realize as they cleared the tables and took down the decorations that "Christmas in the City" would become one of Boston's grandest Christmas parties, the embodiment of the Christmas spirit that Jake and Sparky thought had been lost.

Planning for Christmas in the City begins months before Christmas, when the event's big fund-raiser, its only fund-raiser, takes place, after which Sparky begins roaming the aisles of toy stores, compiling lists of the newest games and gadgets. The lists are sent to shelters where kids select a favorite toy that will be wrapped and personally labeled and waiting for them at the party. But the gift, says Sparky, is the least of what awaits the party guests.

If the red carpet treatment, the twinkling Christmas trees, and a welcome from clowns, magicians, carolers, and hundreds of applauding volunteers isn't exciting enough, there's dinner, more entertainments, and the arrival of Santa atop a cherry picker. But even then, the party is just getting started. Not until the inside walls of the cavernous four-acre hall are drawn back to reveal a winter wonderland—a full-fledged amusement park complete with falling snow, Ferris wheel, merry-go-round, inflatable slides, climbing walls, face painting, a haircutting salon, pony rides, make-your-own gingerbread houses, and a petting zoo of live animals—does Christmas in the City begin to work its magic—on the kids and on the volunteers. The scene is sheer chaos, says Sparky, but an orderly chaos. The children are deliriously happy, some for the first time ever. Their parents, whose every waking moment is spent just trying to survive, weep to see the lighting up of hundreds of faces and hearts.

Christmas in the City is the culmination of a year-round, behind-the-scenes effort by hundreds of unpaid volunteers. More than 2,500 children and 1,200 parents from nearly fifty shelters now attend the lavish party that began so matter-of-factly back in 1989 as a gathering of 165. The 1,500 elves who make the day a success are Kennedy family friends, area high school students, and hundreds more who discover, in the day's outpouring of goodwill and good cheer, the true meaning of Christmas. For Jake and Sparky, few moments in the day are more gratifying than when former "guests," no longer homeless but remembering when a Christmas in the City party gave them or their kids the gift of Christmas love, introduce themselves as volunteers.

Let the Games Begin

FOR MILLIONS of adults, few things evoke the magic of long-ago Christmas mornings like a walk down the aisles of a toy store where, on shelves next to sophisticated computer games and action figures, one can find the classic old board games that have been under every Christmas tree since yesteryear. An enduring part of childhood, they are games that have passed the test of time, and the test of generations of children, the games that have connected one generation, one Christmas, to the next. And many of those games, now played the world over and translated into dozens of foreign languages, had their start in New England.

For generations of children, one game has been the perfect embodiment of Christmas: the deliciously fun, sugarcoated Candyland. With its colorful gingerbread-people markers, its Peppermint Stick Forest, Gum Drop Mountains, King Kandy, Lord Licorice, Lolly and Candy Castle, the color-themed Candyland has been, indeed continues to be, every child's first game—and fantasy world.

In 1949, while recovering from polio, a California woman named Eleanor Abbott created the game of Candyland for children also recovering from the illness. So delighted were children with the colorful playing board and so popular did the game become that Abbott submitted it to the Milton Bradley Company, the Massachusetts-based game maker who packaged Candyland as a "sweet little game . . . for sweet little folks" and sold it for one dollar.

The game pioneer Milton Bradley, a native of Vienna, Maine, had opened his first color lithography shop on Main Street in Springfield, Massachusetts, in 1860. It was not long before he began designing games and puzzles, including The Checkered Game of Life, the earliest family game, whose debut coincided with the dramatic rise of the middle class and its appetite for social entertainment. It was also a time when society was beginning to recognize the needs of children and rethinking its earlier approaches to childhood education.

A generation after Milton Bradley, George Parker founded his own game publishing company in Salem, Massachusetts. Born in 1867, George was the youngest of three brothers, all of whom eventually joined the company. By the late 1880s Parker Brothers had twenty-nine games, most of them invented by George. One game, however, proved more successful than all the others, the game of Monopoly.

Said to have been invented in 1933 by a Pennsylvanian, Charles Darrow, on his kitchen tablecloth, Monopoly was a version of several earlier games based on landlords and real estate in which players could indulge their entrepreneurial spirit. In 1934 Darrow offered Monopoly to Parker Brothers, who tested the game and initially rejected it because of numerous flaws, including the length of time it took to play the game. Not to be discouraged, Darrow had several sets of the game printed for friends and family. Word of the game spread and an avalanche of orders for Monopoly piled in during the 1934 Christmas season. It was the depth of the Great Depression, and, desperate for an escape from economic hardship, people were inspired by the vicarious thrill of financial success that the game offered. By 1935

Parker Brothers had reconsidered its earlier decision and bought the rights
to the game. In no time it became America's best-selling game and a world-
wide phenomenon.

A decade or so before Monopoly made its sensational Parker Brothers
debut, two brothers, Polish immigrants living in Providence, Rhode Island,
were beginning their own company, Hassenfeld Brothers. In 1923 Henry
and Helal Hassenfeld began selling textile remnants, and they later manufactured pencil boxes covered with fabric. Incorporated as Hassenfeld
Brothers Textile Company, the firm expanded to include school supplies,
crayons, and, by the late 1930s, toys. One of those toys, the first toy ever to
be advertised on television and a toy that would find itself under many a
Christmas tree over the next decades, was Mr. Potato Head, Hassenfeld
Brothers' first big toy success.

Invented and patented by George Lerner in 1952, Mr. Potato Head was
based on an earlier make-a-face toy that used real potatoes. The first genial
Mr. Potato Heads by Hassenfeld Brothers included facial features—eyes,
ears, mouths, and noses—as well as a Styrofoam head, though the toy's instructions suggested that a real potato could also be used for all the face-
changing possibilities. By 1960 a plastic potato had been added to the toy

The ever-popular game of Monopoly®. Copyright 2006 by Hasbro, Inc. Used with permission.

and, in short time, Mr. Potato Head became a bona fide star and cherished cultural icon.

In 1984 Hassenfeld Brothers, which changed its name to Hasbro in 1968, acquired the Milton Bradley Company, and in 1991 Parker Brothers joined the Hasbro family. The company continues its New England roots, maintaining corporate offices for its games division in East Longmeadow, Massachusetts, and its toys division in Pawtucket, Rhode Island.

The classic games, those quiet pastimes, continue to work their magic under millions of Christmas trees every year. Hasbro, too, continues to work its own magic every Christmas for thousands of less fortunate children and families who find it difficult to purchase toys and games. Through its charitable programs, the Children's Holiday Fund in Rhode Island and the Children's Giving Tree program in Springfield, Massachusetts, Hasbro makes certain that countless children wake up to a child's garden of fun on Christmas morning.

Dennison Manufacturing: When Your Heart Is in the Gift

IT WAS A manufacturing empire built on paper jewelry boxes, and by the time Dennison Manufacturing Company closed its doors after more than 150 years, it had transformed the way people decorated for Christmas.

The Dennison story begins in the town of Brunswick, Maine, where in 1844 Aaron Dennison set out to make a better and less expensive paper box than the imported box—not always easy to get—that he used in his jewelry business. The first boxes were made by hand, but soon Aaron Dennison had developed a machine to make them. The business thriving, he turned the day-to-day operation over to his brother, Eliphalet Whorf Dennison. By the mid-1850s, Dennison had a salesroom and small factory in Boston. Recognizing that the jewelry business, as well as the woolen trade and retail merchants of all kinds, were in need of better, individualized tags to mark their wares, E. W. Dennison developed what would become the company's signature product—the shipping and merchandise tag. By 1863 Dennison had improved on the tag, patenting the idea of reinforcing the hole on the tag so that it would not easily separate from its package. By 1879 the Brunswick and Boston factories had been consolidated and moved to Framingham, Massachusetts, where for nearly a century Dennison Manufacturing dominated the industrial landscape and earned Framingham the nickname "Tag Town."

There's the
Spirit of
Christmas in
𝒟ennison's
Gift Dressings

A simple gift, properly dressed,
is impressive. If indifference or
lack of thought shows in its
appearance, the gift, however
expensive, is handicapped.
DENNISON'S designs of
Christmas Gift Dressings are
original, artistic and re-
fined; the printing per-
fect, the colors rich.

Ask Your Dealer
for
𝒟ennison's

Christmas Address Tags and
Cards in Red, Gold and Green;
Oval and Round Name Tags;
Christmas Seals; Stamp Seals;
Address and "Express Paid"
Labels, Gift Holders for Bills,
Coins, Gloves and Handkerchiefs;
Coin Boxes, Holly Paper, etc.
Then there are DENNISON
GIFTS—worthy a Dennison
Dressing, unique, high-class, sensible
gifts—Jewelry Cabinets (29 styles),
Jewelry Cleaning Outfits, Handy
Boxes (7 styles), Sealing Wax Sets,
Doll Outfits, etc. And not to be
forgotten are **Dennison Table
and Room Decorations,** all of
paper, inexpensive and effective.

𝒟ennison's Christmas Book

pictures and tells about them all.
May we send you a free copy?
Address Dept. "I." at our nearest store.

𝒟ennison Manufacturing Company
The Tag Makers

By the turn of the twentieth century, with salesrooms in major American cities and with the growing popularity of Christmas, Dennison Manufacturing recognized an opportunity to transform the way that people celebrate Christmas. Gifts had been simple and homemade, wrapped, if at all, in plain brown paper with sealing wax and twine. Industrialization, however, had flooded the marketplace with mass-produced, inexpensive goods tailored to the growing middle class and to specific family members. Department stores, in an effort to boost sales, began showing off their new merchandise in decorated store windows. The appeal of the merchandise was enhanced by its being wrapped in the new tissues and crepe papers. A gift's appeal thus became a gift in itself.

Hoping to nurture an appreciation for beautiful packages, Dennison Manufacturing created a line of gift "dressings"—tags, bows, ribbons, wrap, seals, and tissue—for thoughtful and imaginative gift wrapping. Dennison, whose high standards in materials as well as design were always a company hallmark, believed that one paid friends and family members a special compliment by wrapping *for* them individually. "When your heart is in the gift," gushed the company advertising, Dennison was the choice.

To instruct people on how to achieve a holiday atmosphere at home, in church, and in school, Dennison published a line of sweetly and charmingly illustrated how-to books in the 1910s and 1920s. In essence product catalogs, the books were filled with ideas for lighting the home, bow making, centerpieces, tree decorations, pageant costumes, and party games, all of which could be accomplished with Dennison paper products.

Dennison Manufacturing Company
advertisement, 1909. Private collection.

Throughout the twentieth century, Dennison continued to be the pioneering and innovative company it had always been, adding hundreds of new products every year to a line that numbered some ten thousand in the company's heyday. The success of the Christmas product line spawned other holiday lines that became one of the five major divisions of the company. In 1990 Dennison merged with label maker Avery and in 1993 relocated to California.

E. W. Dennison had built his company on a simple philosophy handed down from his father: "Whatever is worth doing at all is worth doing well." And every Christmas, that legacy is remembered when a gift is carefully chosen and lovingly wrapped—with one's heart inside.

New England Seafarers Mission: A Ditty Bag Christmas

DURING THE Christmas season, while many are taking a moment from their busy lives to reflect and renew, seafarers around the world are spending Christmas at work, far from loved ones. For Bosnian, Filipino, Indonesian, Ukrainian, Romanian, and German seamen arriving in New England ports to deliver sugar, cars, and fuel, the loneliness of being away from home is made all the more acute by the joyous sights and sounds of Christmas, reminders that their families and friends are together at home, sharing the blessings of the season.

Although there may be no place like home for the holidays, the chaplain and volunteers of the New England Seafarers Mission do their best to be "family," making Boston and other New England ports safe havens that feel a little bit like home. Founded in 1880 by Olaus Olson, a Swedish sailor who knew well the hardships—physical and psychological—of a life at sea, the New England Seafarers Mission has stayed the course for more than a century, serving the needs, spiritual and physical, of seamen aboard cruise and industrial ships. Every small act of assistance that helps to uplift the spirit— an encouraging word or a shared prayer, a Bible in a native tongue, a phone card that connects a seaman to his child, a wire service that sends desperately needed money home—reveals the presence of God, and his message that he loves and cares for each person.

And at Christmastime, that message can be found in a bulging sack, slung on the shoulder of the port chaplain, who, doing his best imitation of Santa Claus, visits ships to deliver ditty bags.

The Christmas Ditty Bag project is a yearlong labor of love for members of the Women's Seafarers Friend Society, an organization of church groups from New England, New Jersey, Pennsylvania, and Minnesota who support the New England Seafarers Mission. Organized in 1895 during the era of sailing ships, the Women's Seafarers Friend Society once provided social and educational assistance to seafaring families, cared for and ministered to sick and injured sailors in hospitals, and supplied clothing and food for shipwrecked sailors.

By 1972, with the maritime industry changing, the group began devoting its energies to preparing handmade ditty bags, once called comfort bags, for crews that visit the New England ports of Boston, Providence, Portsmouth, and Portland during the Christmas season. That first year, fifty ditty bags were prepared. Today more than two hundred women work all year assembling needle-and-thread mending kits, stitching drawstring bags, knitting hats, and collecting such sundries as razors, clippers, socks, candy, gum, cocoa, and noodle soup. In late November many of the compassionate volunteers gather for roll-up day, the day when T-shirts donated by various New England organizations are neatly folded and rolled for packing. A week later the women reconvene for packing day, and by lunchtime more than 1,800 ditty bags—each with a Christmas prayer for safety and a personal Christmas greeting enclosed—are packed and ready for delivery throughout New England. By January 6, the feast of the Epiphany, all will be distributed onboard to ships' captains or first mates.

Some crews will use the ditty bags to usher in the day with a celebration they would not have had otherwise. For many seamen who receive ditty bags, it will be their first Christmas gift in years, the first time in a long time that they've had a moment and a reason to pause and reflect on the day. They may ask to hear the Christmas story, or a prayer. Not everyone who receives a ditty bag is Christian, but it doesn't matter. God's love is for everyone and the ditty bag, filled with the kindness of strangers, is a tangible expression of that love.

O Little Town of Bethlehem

EVERY DECEMBER something magical happens in the little town of Bethlehem, Connecticut. Thousands of people come from all over New England with stacks and boxes of Christmas mail in hand. They make their way to the Bethlehem Post Office on East Street to receive the town's blessing for the season—a decorative rubber stamp endorsement, called a cachet, for their Christmas cards and letters.

Another Bethlehem

Like Bethlehem, Connecticut, the township of Bethlehem, New Hampshire, incorporated on December 25, 1799, has its own special postal

The cachet created for Bethlehem, New Hampshire.
Courtesy Bethlehem, New Hampshire, Post Office.

cachet that is applied to cards during the month of December. Created more than fifty years ago by a town resident, the cachet depicts the little town of Bethlehem on a hillside surrounded by evergreens.

The tradition of cacheting cards and letters began in this Litchfield Hills town—population 3,500—in 1938, when Postmaster Earl Johnson designed the first cachet for a Christmas greeting he sent to President Franklin Roosevelt. It may have been that he was only hoping that his card would stand out from the mountain of mail the White House received, but he unwittingly began a tradition that continues today.

A selection of cachets used over the years. The first one designed is at top left.
Courtesy Bethlehem, Connecticut, Post Office.

That first cachet, a simple Christmas tree topped by a star, included the message "From the Little Town of BETHLEHEM CHRISTMAS GREETINGS." The following year a new design from the "Christmas Town" was offered to postal patrons. Every year since, schoolchildren, local residents, area artists, and post office employees submit designs—from Santas and hollies, lambs and Wise Men, to angels, doves, reindeer, and mangers—the only requirement for which is that the design include the words *Bethlehem, Connecticut* or *The Christmas Town.*

One design is chosen each year and made into a rubber stamp, and with all the previous years' cachets, the new design is made available, in the lobby of the post office, to the general public during the month of December. And while walk-in patrons are busy doing their own stamping, postal employees are trying to keep pace with the parcels of officially stamped cards and letters that arrive daily from all over the world, all awaiting their special decorative stamp. The mood is festive, with Christmas music playing all day, and if the pace is just a little bit frantic for the postal workers, you'll never hear them complain. They'll work seven days a week during December, with extended daily hours much of the month, and they'll process more than 225,000 Christmas cards and letters in a twenty-four-day period, more mail than during the other eleven months combined. They know they are part of a beloved Bethlehem tradition, know that at any moment a young child may walk through the doors to stamp her very first card and begin her own tradition, or that a senior citizen may drop in to continue a tradition begun fifty years earlier.

Preparing Christmas Greens, by T. De Thulstrup. From *Harper's Weekly*, 1880. Courtesy Dover Publications.

V. Lights and Decorations

SINCE PREHISTORIC TIMES, a light in the dark has been a source of warmth and comfort, a symbol of hope. For the ancient peoples of Europe, light was life, especially during the midwinter season, when the sun was at its weakest. Bonfires, torch fires, and hearth fires were lit as imitative magic to coax the life-giving sun back to strength.

Decorations, too, played an important role in ancient midwinter festivals. Homes were bedecked in holly, ivy, and mistletoe. Though all trees were worshipped as sacred, sentient beings, the evergreen had an honored place, and the hanging of objects on its boughs was believed to enhance health and fortune and to prophesy whatever the object symbolized. Gilded nuts, straw ornaments, and fruits—especially apples, which represented the sacred orchards—were tied to branches as offerings to the agricultural gods. Shiny metal objects that reflected light honored the sun gods. At the conclusion of the midwinter festival, the sacred greens were burned in ritual.

Christians adapted the fires and decorations of the midwinter festival to celebrate the birth of Christ. Torches and lanterns guided the faithful to church, where Christmas candles burned throughout Christmas Day, their smoke twirling heavenward. When Christmas was outlawed during the Puritan reign, Irish families continued the tradition of placing a candle in a window of their homes on Christmas Eve, as a sign to the parish priest that the celebration of midnight Mass would be welcome. The candle's light also served as a sign of hospitality and comfort to wayfarers who might be in need of shelter or food.

During the Victorian era, objects with ancient pagan symbolism became popular Christmas tree decorations. Paper cornucopias—horns of plenty representing abundance—and eggshell baskets representing birds' nests held confections and nuts. Gingerbread boys were hung from the tips of branches and strings of popcorn garlanded boughs.

Massachusetts State House decorated for Christmas, 1932.
Courtesy Bostonian Society/Old State House.

Today, across New England, cities and towns shimmer at Christmastime with decorative light displays that delight young and old alike. Lantern tours and candlelight strolls at many of New England's historic sites and living-history museums not only provide a glimpse into Christmases past, but also draw people out of their cozy homes and into the comfort and embrace of others.

Candlelight Strolls: Old Sturbridge Village and Strawbery Banke

IT IS NO WONDER that for years visitors to two of New England's premier living-history museums—Old Sturbridge Village and Strawbery Banke— had expressed an interest in visiting the sites during the Christmas season. They imagined that the quiet beauty of the villages, the quaint lanes and historic buildings, would be the perfect backdrop for an old-fashioned Christmas. But curators—sticklers for historical accuracy—had a dilemma: how to re-create an old-fashioned Christmas where and when there had been no Christmas.

For Old Sturbridge Village, a re-created rural 1838 New England community, Puritan influence, though waning, would still have permeated day-to-day life. At Strawbery Banke and its Puddle Dock neighborhood on Portsmouth's Piscataqua River, a neighborhood that had evolved over more than three centuries, only two of the nineteenth-century buildings would have displayed Christmas decorations. Like so many other places across New England, Portsmouth had in its early years been heavily influenced by Puritan values.

The solution for curators at both sites was not to re-create a Christmas that never was, but to use the historic settings to *interpret* the evolution and history of Christmas traditions. Christmas Traditions by Candlelight is a magical evening stroll through the lantern-lined streets of festively— though simply—decorated Old Sturbridge Village that takes in the sights, sounds, and scents of a nineteenth-century Christmas. It is an opportunity, during the hectic Christmas season, to pause momentarily and consider the beginnings of our traditions—the stockings, mistletoe, holiday foods, greeting cards, and Santa Claus—and to discover why we do what we do every December. Why are there fruitcakes, plum puddings, peppermint sticks, and wassail? Why are roasted chestnuts and spicy gingerbread so much a part of the season?

At the Center Meetinghouse, the symbol of Sturbridge's community spirit, musical performances explore caroling traditions. In 1838 America was on the cusp of becoming a consumer society, and the Knight Store is stocked with a variety of plain, fancy, and exotic goods—teas and textiles, spices and seeds, citrus and candies. Oranges, books, costume jewelry, and small toys—including Jacob's ladders and cup-and-ball games—would become favorite gifts for Christmas giving. At the stately and elegant Salem

Make a Paper Cornucopia Ornament

WHAT YOU WILL NEED: Scissors; glue stick; gift wrap in various designs and patterns (firmer papers work best); curling ribbon; small candies and nuts

To make your cornucopia:

1. Cut 5 x 5-inch squares from the various patterns of gift wrap.
2. Cut 3 x 3-inch squares from other gift wrap patterns that complement your larger squares.
3. Cut pieces of the ribbon in 8-inch lengths.
4. With one of the large squares in the diamond position, with its design face down, make a loop with a length of ribbon and glue it in the corner of the square. This will be your ornament hanger (figure A).
5. Take one of your small squares and glue it face up to the corner of the large square, over the ribbon (figure B).

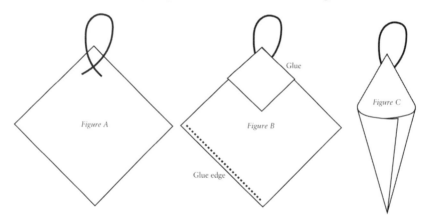

6. Run a bead of glue along the lower left edge of the large square and fold the paper into a cone shape with the ends slightly overlapping. Press the seam together (figure C).
7. Fill your cornucopia with small candies and nuts and hang on your Christmas tree.

—Instructions courtesy of Old Sturbridge Village

Towne House, a home that reflects the prosperity of the emerging business class, gift giving and charitable giving are traced from their seventeenth-century beginnings, when the poor went from house to house asking for holiday food and drink.

Father Christmas makes an appearance at the Bullard Tavern, where visitors can listen to a hearthside reading of Clement Clarke Moore's beloved *Visit from St. Nicholas,* take a few turns on the dance floor accompanied by fiddles and tin whistles, and make cornucopias. At the Fitch House visitors share in the re-creation of the first New England Christmas tree—Charles Follen's tree—a modest tabletop tree colorfully decorated with tin icicles, wax tapers, and cornucopias and eggshell baskets filled with small candies and gilded nuts.

In Portsmouth, Strawbery Banke's Candlelight Stroll began in 1979 as part of a Christmas craft fair. For the stroll, more than a dozen of the museum's historic buildings are open and decorated. Luminarias, set in hand-made lanterns, light the friendly lanes and guide visitors through the centuries and the lives of the people from the Puddle Dock neighborhood. Over at the Revolutionary War–era tavern, a few sprigs of greenery hint at the season, but it is business as usual on the chilly December evening. At the Chase House, exotic fruit pyramids, gilded nuts, figs, and plates of teacakes grace the table. Dried floral arrangements, wreaths, kissing balls, and swags reflect the holiday traditions of a well-to-do family in 1818.

At the Goodwin Mansion, Christmas finds its fullest, most lavish 1870s Victorian expression. All the newest trends are on display. Fragrant, beribboned greens fill the house. Tables are heavy with meringues and marzipan and gingerbreads. Piles of gifts, a reflection of the new consumer society, are colorfully wrapped. The Christmas tree is decorated with cornucopias filled with sweet treats and nuts, with tinsel and hand-blown glass ornaments from Germany.

At the Shapiro House, Mrs. Shapiro, a Russian Jewish immigrant from Ukraine, is celebrating the 1919 holiday season with potato latkes, a game of dreidel, and the lighting of the menorah. And at the World War II–era Abbott Store, folks on the home front in 1943 are doing their best to stay in the holiday spirit by packing small necessities for loved ones away at war.

Like other events at living-history museums throughout New England, Christmas Traditions by Candlelight and Candlelight Stroll are opportunities to share an evening of fellowship, not only with friends and neighbors, but with all who walked the streets in earlier times, and to remember who we are, from where we've come, and the traditions and sentiments we collectively share.

Nubble Light: A Beacon of Hope

As long as Christians have looked to Christmas for comfort and hope, mariners have looked to lighthouses to guide them safely home. What began more than two thousand years ago as purely functional aids to navigation, alerting mariners to dangers at sea, are now romantic icons of a glorious maritime past. Over the centuries, the lighthouse has shone its way into ghostly tales of mystery and stories of human tragedy and triumph. The arresting aloofness and dignified simplicity of the lighthouse, a symbol of reliability and strength, appeals to mariner and landlubber alike.

They come in all sizes, shapes, and design, and for every lighthouse that sits isolated on a dangerous ledge far out to sea, there is another, accessible from the mainland, on a bluff or breakwater. But few are as tantalizingly close, seemingly in reach—and yet so far away—as the Cape Neddick Light, the jewel of York, Maine. The light is fondly known as Nubble Light because of its location on the small, rocky island—the nubble—a mere one hundred yards across a channel off the Cape Neddick peninsula. The story is often told of the lighthouse cat—a master mouser—who regularly swam the narrow but treacherous channel for off-island visits with friends.

The first talk of building a light station on the rocky outcropping in the shadow of Bald Head Cliff was heard in 1807, but it would be another seventy years before Congress appropriated the money and construction began. On July 1, 1879, the light station was dedicated and its kerosene lamp lighted for the first time by the United States Lighthouse Service. When the Lighthouse Service was phased out in 1939, the Coast Guard took over Nubble Light. By 1987 the light had been automated and the last keeper had come ashore. Ownership of the light passed to the Town of York, where today it is maintained by the dedicated Friends of Nubble Light.

Beginning in the early 1980s, with lights donated by a local resident, Margaret Cummings, in memory of her sister, Nubble Light was dressed up for Christmas by its keepers. In 1987 another York resident, Verna Rundlett, turned the lighting of the Nubble into an official Christmas event, one that has only brightened over the years. Today wreaths are hung on buildings

The National Shrine of Our Lady of LaSalette

On September 19, 1846, an apparition of the Virgin Mary is said to have appeared to two young cow herders, Melanie and Maximin, atop a mountain in the French Alps parish of LaSalette. The children were frightened by the vision until she told them to come closer, that they had nothing to fear.

The Garden of St. Francis of Assisi at the National Shrine of Our Lady of LaSalette. Private collection.

Mary spoke to the children sympathetically, telling them of the world's apathy toward the church. She said that God's commandments and the Sabbath were being broken, the Lord's name was being taken in vain. With sorrow, she told the children that if the world did not turn away from evil, blight would come to the crops and starvation to the people. But if the people repented, the fields would flourish, the potatoes would sow themselves, and the stones would turn into wheat.

Mary encouraged the children to spread her message of reconciliation. They made it their mission and after five years of investigation, the bishop of Grenoble deemed the apparition of the Blessed Virgin authentic. In 1852 the order of the Missionaries of Our Lady of LaSalette was founded in France, and by 1892 missionaries had arrived in Hartford, Connecticut, from which Mary's message spread across America.

In 1942 the order established a seminary in Attleboro, Massachusetts. By 1952 construction had begun on the LaSalette Shrine, and on December 8, 1953, the shrine celebrated its first Christmas with several thousand lights and several thousand pilgrims. In the years since, the outdoor Christmas Festival of Lights has grown to more than 300,000 dazzling lights that illuminate the Holy Stairs, the Garden of the Apparition, the Rosary Walk, the Garden of St. Francis of Assisi, and the trees that reach to the heavenly lights.

and a lighted Christmas tree sparkles from behind the window of the keeper's house. The forty-one-foot lighthouse and its distinctive red oil house, outlined in white lights, are the centerpiece of York's Christmas celebration.

One of the most photographed lighthouses in America, the Nubble is radiant both at Christmas and in July, when it is again bejeweled for summer visitors to kick off the annual York Days celebration, which draws thousands of visitors from near and far. On the Saturday after Thanksgiving, the faithful brave the chilly air and biting winds to gather at Sohier Park, just across the narrow channel from the Nubble, to sing carols and drink hot chocolate. As dark descends, the tower's 2,500-candlepower beacon flashes fifteen miles out across an icy sea, and the countdown begins. Nubble's white Christmas lights are switched on, glowing against a backdrop of velvet black, a reminder of a time when the night was lit only from the heavens and stars showed the way. Once a beacon of hope for sailors, Nubble Light has been reborn as a beacon of hope during the darkest days of the midwinter season.

Mystic Seaport: Christmas by the Sea

IN OCTOBER 1929 Americans watched helplessly as the stock market collapsed and the economy unraveled. As panic set in, so too did the realization that the future might not be safe, that a way of life so many had enjoyed might be slipping away.

That same year, on Christmas Day, concerned citizens in Mystic, Connecticut, gathered to contemplate the seaport's future. Though a small port, for three hundred years Mystic had been a significant shipbuilding center. With a proud seafaring tradition, Mystic could claim to have launched a greater tonnage of ships than any other port of comparable size in America.

But that heritage—the wooden ships, the nautical arts and skills, the seafaring way of life, and the romance of the sea—seemed also to be slipping away in 1929, until Edward E. Bradley, an industrialist, Carl C. Cutler, a lawyer, and Dr. Charles K. Stillman, a physician, founded the Marine Historical Association to preserve America's maritime traditions and educate the public about America's relationship with the sea. If there was little optimism elsewhere in America during the Christmas of 1929, the citizens of Mystic had much to be hopeful about. They saw their historic seaport as a symbol of rebirth.

By 1931 donations of maritime artifacts were pouring into Mystic, and by the early 1940s the association had acquired the *Charles W. Morgan*, the nation's last wooden whaleship, as well as historic buildings from across New England that were moved to Mystic to re-create an authentic seaside village, complete with costumed interpreters and skilled artisans who reflected nineteenth-century New England life.

For more than a quarter of a century, visitors have stepped into a nineteenth-century New England Christmas during Mystic Seaport's annual Lantern Light Tours. The tours, moving plays of magic, merriment, and mystery, are led by costumed guides who take visitors by lantern light to various locations in the village where scenes are played out. Visitors can eavesdrop on the latest comings and goings—even the gossip—of the village as it prepares for Christmas.

The year may be 1876. Families are gathering for Christmas Eve, putting the finishing touches on their celebration. One German family, newly arrived in America, has gathered in the parlor to open a special package of hand-blown glass ornaments sent from relatives back home. Another family is nervously awaiting the outcome of its Christmas table centerpiece, an old-fashioned English plum pudding whose preparation began a week earlier. Outside, in the narrow, dark streets, villagers hurry home, greeting one another cheerily. On the town green, bundled-up carolers sing one of the new holiday songs, "One-Horse Open Sleigh," and the strains from a squeezebox can be heard from the tavern. Voices drift out into the streets from the dark recesses of the waterfront, where, in his quarters on a ship, a sailor reads a letter by candlelight. Woven through the scenes is the delicious intrigue of the evening's magical story, whose happy resolution comes at the end.

Christmas is not a time nor a season, but a state of mind. To cherish peace and goodwill, to be plenteous in mercy, is to have the real spirit of Christmas.

—Calvin Coolidge

The historically accurate tour changes each year and a cast of more than 120 players brings the village and its residents to vivid life. Visitors can share a song or kick up their heels in the tavern. They can nibble on a gingersnap and take a ride in a horse-drawn omnibus. Mystic Seaport Lantern Light Tours are a respite from the hustle and bustle of the modern Christmas, a rare opportunity to indulge in the quieter moments of the season and to let oneself be absorbed by the past.

A Nantucket Noel: Killen Dory

NANTUCKET—like Stowe, Vermont, Wiscasset, Maine, Newport, Rhode Island, Portsmouth, New Hampshire, and Boston's Louisburg Square —was described by one writer of yesteryear as a shrine town, a preserved village that does not reconstruct old Yankee life but, instead, lives it daily.

An elbow of sand, fourteen miles long and lying thirty miles out to sea off the Massachusetts coast, Nantucket takes its name from the Native American Wampanoag word for "faraway land." First a refuge for Native Americans, then Quakers, Nantucket became the "whaling capital of the world" during the heyday of whaling, from 1750 to 1830, when nearly two hundred vessels made the island their home port.

The decline of the whaling industry during the late nineteenth century left islanders with little livelihood until summer visitors, eager for respite, began arriving from the mainland for the invigorating sea air, the wild moors, cranberry bogs, pristine beaches, and cobblestone streets. Nantucket's isolation had served it well, preserving its charm and beauty as well as hundreds of pre–Civil War homes. As summer homes were built and pleasure boats began crowding the harbor where whaling ships had once anchored, Nantucket, little changed since the eighteenth century, became one of New England's premier vacation destinations—in and off season.

If this gem of an island, so steeped in tradition and history, now shines year-round, it is never more luminous than at Christmastide, when the cobblestones are dusted with snow, the lamplights are lit, and historic homes, decorated with fresh greens, berries, pinecones, and seashells, sparkle for the monthlong, old-fashioned Nantucket Noel celebration.

Beginning the day after Thanksgiving and continuing until New Year's Eve, every corner of Nantucket echoes with the spirit of a Dickensian Christmas. Festivities begin the first weekend after Thanksgiving with the Christmas Stroll, tree lightings, and the arrival of Santa Claus on a Coast Guard

Leaving Brighton Hotel for the Milldam, 1871. Courtesy Boston Athenaeum.

The Longfellows' Christmas tree, as painted by Edith Longfellow, 1862.
Courtesy National Park Service, Longfellow National Historic Site.

Topping off at a construction site, with the ceremonial evergreen and flag, 2005. Photo by David L. Ryan, courtesy The Boston Globe Store.

Nova Scotia's gift of a Christmas tree arrives in Boston. Courtesy Harron and Associates.

A winter hayride at The Rocks Christmas Tree Farm. Photo by Kindra Kline, courtesy The Rocks Christmas Tree Farm, Bethlehem, New Hampshire.

The Killen family's Christmas dory. Photo by H. Flint Ranney.

The illuminated Pilgrim Monument in Provincetown. Photo by David Atkinson, courtesy of the Pilgrim Monument and Provincetown Museum.

Lobster pot Christmas tree, Cape Porpoise, Maine. Courtesy Robert Dennis/www.portimages.com.

Stockings hung by the chimney at Old Sturbridge Village. Courtesy Old Sturbridge Village Christmas Traditions by Candlelight, Sturbridge, Massachusetts.

(ABOVE) Luminarias light the way at Strawbery Banke. Courtesy Strawbery Banke Candlelight Stroll, Portsmouth, New Hampshire.

(LEFT) Mystic Seaport Lantern Light Tours. Courtesy Mystic Seaport, Mystic, Connecticut.

Children on Sleds, by Louis Prang, c. 1885. Courtesy Prang Collection, Boston Public Library Print Department.

Xmas postcard, 1911. Private collection.

(LEFT) *Christmas Morning, before Daylight,* by Kellogg and Bulkeley Lithographer, after 1871. Courtesy Connecticut Historical Society.

(BELOW LEFT) The sign that hangs outside Clement C. Moore's former home, Newport, Rhode Island. Private collection.

(BELOW) *Children Singing in Window,* by Louis Prang, c. 1885. Courtesy Prang Collection, Boston Public Library Print Department.

(ABOVE) Folk art Christmas rug. Copyright Shelburne Museum, Shelburne, Vermont.

(RIGHT) An eggnog recipe card by Peter Hunt, c. 1940. Courtesy Lynn Van Dine/The Search for Peter Hunt.

(BELOW) Mr. Potato Head.® Copyright 2006 Hasbro, Inc. Used with permission.

6 eggs

5 spoons of sugar

a little of rye

a bottle of rum

a pint of cream

a pint of milk

Eggnog

makes a Merry Christmas

Peter Hunt

(ABOVE) Nubble Light and outbuildings outlined in white lights against the night sky, York, Maine. Photo by Jeremy D'Entremont.

(LEFT) The Polar Express Santa holds high the first gift of Christmas. Courtesy A. O. Lucy/Lucy Marketing.

vessel. For the next four weeks, carolers and musicians in Victorian costume stroll the streets. There are walking tours of the quaint town, concerts, community caroling, artist demonstrations, charity raffles, holiday parties, pet photos with Santa, cookie decorating, bell ringing, a Festival of Wreaths at Preservation Hall, and a Festival of Trees at the Whaling Museum. Theater companies perform *A Child's Christmas in Wales, The Tailor of Gloucester,* and readings from *A Christmas Carol.*

If Nantucket Noel brings a special glow to the island, one family's own simple, elegant expression of the season has become, over the years, every islander's tradition. It was back in 1965 that Sidney Killen surprised his wife, Ann, on their first Christmas together with a small, lighted Christmas tree, set in a dory and anchored in the Easy Street Basin, across the street from the Killen home. The tiny tree glowed against the harbor's dark backdrop. It was, Ann remembers, a "small, sweet, creative Christmas decoration, a personal thing" that would, over time, become an icon of Nantucket's Christmas season.

In the years since Sidney's inspiration, the Killen family Christmas dory has enchanted not only islanders but also thousands of Christmastime visitors to Nantucket who get their first glimpse of the dory and tree from the island ferry and then make their way down to the Easy Street Basin for a closer look. Storms have tossed the little boat, which has had to be rebuilt once, and winds have flickered the tiny colored lights, but the tree has always been there, for forty years, a welcome in the dark. The secret to the tree's appeal, believes Ann Killen, is its simplicity, and the letters she receives every year from visitors who have enjoyed the decoration make her feel that her family's tradition is, in a small way, a part of everyone's Christmas. Ann's grandchildren are now in charge of the tree and though she travels off-island for much of the year, Ann is always home for Christmas, enjoying the floating tradition, as she always has, from her living room window.

ChemArt: Keepsakes Etched in Time

As Christianity spread, Christmas Eve miracle plays dramatized the lessons from the Bible and used evergreen boughs, hung with apples, to symbolize the Tree of Paradise in the Garden of Eden. The popularity of medieval miracle plays inspired people to use evergreens in their own homes, but not until the mid-nineteenth century, when Queen Victoria and Prince Albert lavishly decorated an evergreen at Windsor Castle, did the

Christmas tree capture the fancy and imagination of the public. Adorned with gilded nuts and gingerbreads, candies and fruits, the "sugar tree" became each family's individual creation and personal expression of the season. No two trees were alike, as families added ribbons, paper flowers, strings of beads, penny toys, and straw ornaments to the sugary edibles.

By the early twentieth century, the availability of mass-produced, affordable, generic glass ornaments from Germany was changing the way many families decorated. Sold in five-and-dimes such as Woolworth's, the icicles and shiny, reflective colored balls replaced many of the unique handmade ornaments; one family's tree began to look very much like everyone else's. In recent years, though, the trend has been away from generic ornaments and back to homemade decorations and keepsake ornaments that capture personal family memories and moments. And one New England company, ChemArt, is creating those Christmas keepsakes, turning Christmas trees once again into memory trees that shine with the ageless beauty of designs etched in time.

Tucked away in a quiet corner of an industrial park in Lincoln, Rhode Island, ChemArt captures life's special moments for dozens of private clients, including nonprofits, universities, historical societies, and government agencies that use the sale of personalized, gold-finished ornaments to fund educational, conservation, and historic projects. Fewer than 10 percent of ornaments are now made in the United States, but ChemArt continues to defy the trend to move overseas. Founded by Dick Beaupre in East Providence in 1976, ChemArt employs eighty—a workforce that doubles during the holiday season—for whom every day in Lincoln, Rhode Island, is Christmas. Indeed, visitors to the company will find a trimmed Christmas tree—a dazzling display of ChemArt's creations—in the lobby, not just at Christmas, but every day of the year.

What ends as an ornament that captures and reflects all the light and sentimentality of the season begins, prosaically enough, with a thin sheet of smooth-polished brass. It's not long, though, before the magic of the photochemical etching process begins, first with lamination and then with a sandwiching of the elegant design, readying the brass for exposure and development, the first steps in a seventeen-step process. The etching process cuts away tiny sections of the metal, after which the ornament is electrostatically plated with nickel and finished with twenty-four-karat gold. A silkscreenlike process adds delicate spots of color—as many as ten colors on an intricate piece—and the ornament is ready for assembly. It may be that the real magic takes place during the assembly process. All ChemArt ornaments are made on the flat sheets of brass, but during assembly the flat pieces are layered and sculpted to give the ornament its three dimensions. For added elegance and color, cameo-like resin and porcelain designs are often incorporated into the brass design.

If, with its popular line of Baldwin ornaments, its nature, tropical, and flower series, and its sports collections, ChemArt preserves the everyday, individual family events worthy of celebration, so, too, do ChemArt's custom ornaments celebrate our national heritage, the memories of the collective family of Americans.

In 1981 ChemArt's unique design and etching process caught the eye of the White House Historical Association (WHHA), a nonprofit organization begun in 1961 by First Lady Jacqueline Kennedy to enhance public understanding, appreciation, and enjoyment of the White House and to preserve its treasured heirlooms. To commemorate the presidents, the White House Historical Association inaugurated an ornament series, selecting ChemArt to manufacture the ornaments and launching the series with a simple, elegant angel fashioned after an early American weathervane made in 1840 in Charlestown, Massachusetts, for the Universalist Church in Newburyport, Massachusetts. Since that first ornament the designs, beginning in 1982 with an ornament celebrating the 250th anniversary of George Washington's birth, have chronologically honored the presidents as well as landmark anniversaries.

Angel ornament, 1981. Courtesy ChemArt.

Privileged to have manufactured the White House ornament—the original of which hangs each season on the White House Christmas tree in the Blue Room—since 1981 and to have designed all but five of the ornaments over the years, ChemArt creates a keepsake that reflects not only the presidency but the man and his family and their ties to the Christmas season. Since its premier ornament, several subsequent WHHA ornaments have had ties to New England. The 1983 ornament, a miniature replica of the north facade of the White House, commemorated the presidency of John Adams; in 1987 his son, John Quincy Adams, was honored. In 1997 the Christmas ornament commemorated the restoration and redecoration of the White House during the administration of New Hampshire's Franklin Pierce.

For years, knowing little if anything about ChemArt, collectors of ornaments—and memories—have cherished the company's unique creations, sold under the private labels and the renowned Baldwin name. But ChemArt is poised to emerge from its behind-the-scenes role with new designs and ornaments, including its Santa's Garden—a collection of floral ornaments and seed packs in a postcard mailer—that will be sold under the ChemArt name.

Christmas, in one sense, is a deeply personal time that means something different to everyone, but it is also a time when the human family collectively reflects on the year, and the years, past. If, over time, memories and sentiments become more difficult to hold on to, they are made a little more tangible by the lustrous beauty of the ornaments we hang on our trees.

VI. Music, Art, and Literature

THE SONGS WE SING at Christmas have their origins in the ancient round dances, accompanied by flutes and performed year-round during seasonal agricultural rituals and processionals to ensure the health and fertility of the crops.

One of the most sacred of the midwinter agricultural processionals was the honoring—wassailing—of fruit trees, particularly apple trees. Villagers were led by firelight to the orchard, where one tree was chosen to represent the orchard. From the wassail bowl villagers drank a toast of mulled cider or ale to the tree—*Waes Hael,* meaning good health—and splashed wassail on its roots. Women and children danced—symbolizing the life force—and sang folksongs with repetitive verses so as to encourage a bountiful crop. They paraded from house to house with the wassail bowl and with baskets of apples, evergreens, and dollies made from corn husks, which represented the sun, rebirth, and the harvest.

Early Christians condemned ritual folk carols as the devil's dancing and replaced them with theological Latin hymns and chants. Sung by the celebrant, not the congregation, hymns and chants were filled with piety and praise designed to teach doctrine. In the thirteenth century, when St. Francis of Assisi introduced joyful song and dance around his life-sized Nativity, he ushered in a golden age of popular carols, festive carols for the people. The songs, derived from ancient feasting processionals, were written in the vernacular by poets of the day to celebrate Mary, the Christ child, and the saints. The church tried to suppress the songs, which were sung throughout the year, and the singing of them by entire congregations, but by the sixteenth century the carols were well established across Europe.

With the Puritan condemnation of Christmas, it appeared by the nineteenth century that the old carols had been lost and forgotten. But in small, isolated villages the folksongs endured, spread by wandering minstrels and passed down through families. Victorian folklorists and antiquarians began collecting the carols and by the time Charles Dickens was "reinventing" Christmas, the olds songs were not only experiencing their own renaissance, but also inspiring a new golden age of Christmas music. In time, the word *carol* became associated exclusively with the songs of Christmas and with the custom of singing—caroling—in the open air on Christmas Eve.

Caroling was born of the "waits," the night watchmen of old walled English cities. Waits patrolled the streets, marking the hours with their musical instruments. They also performed at social events. By the early nineteenth century, as towns and cities began to establish professional police forces to patrol the streets, waits were dismissed from their posts and many began traveling the countryside, serenading the public in the tradition of ancient wassailers. Later, small groups of costumed carolers—who also became known as waits—took up the tradition and began assembling on town greens, banishing the cold and dark and imparting warmth and comfort with their songs and handbell ringing.

If the songs of Christmas have their roots in age-old traditions, so, too, do bells. At one time little more than small, crude noisemakers made of metal, clay, or wood, bells were believed to possess strange and spiritual powers. They were rung to keep evil and darkness at bay, to alter the weather, and to ensure a bountiful crop in the coming season. They were hung on trees to alert homeowners to the presence of nature sprites. They were buried near graves in the hopes of resurrecting the dead and hung in doorways to keep homes safe from any evil that might be waiting to slip in with visitors. They were worn as amulets to protect people and animals from plague and pestilence, thunder and lightning. Later, bells were used to mark time, to summon help, to bring people together, to signal the approach of sleighs, and to ring the message of freedom across the land.

Now associated with Christmas and Christianity, the use of bells in churches began in the sixth century. Bells were baptized as living beings and hung high in towers, suspended between heaven and earth, symbolic of the communication between God and man. Their clappers, it was said, were the tongues of angels, announcing happy and sad events.

At no time are the tintinnabulations of bells more welcome than on a frosty Christmas Eve, when handbells ring out the ancient tunes, or on Christmas morning, when bells in white steeples, pealing out a message of fellowship, call the faithful to worship.

Christmas carolers at the Old State House, 1921. Courtesy Bostonian Society/Old State House.

Five Men Making Music

THREE WERE MEN of the cloth, another was the son of a Unitarian minister. One was an honored and popular poet. Four were New England natives. The other, though born in Pennsylvania, grew up in Vermont. All were born within twenty-eight years and died within seventeen years of each other. And, all, within a creative period of eighteen years, wrote songs that have become cherished standards for the Christmas season.

Henry Wadsworth Longfellow, 1865.
Courtesy National Park Service,
Longfellow National Historic Site.

The distinguished elder of the five was Henry Wadsworth Longfellow. Born in 1807 in Portland, Maine, into a prominent family, Longfellow taught at Bowdoin and Harvard Colleges before retiring in 1854 to devote his time to writing. His famous epic poems drew on episodes from history: *Evangeline: A Tale of Acadie, The Song of Hiawatha, The Courtship of Miles Standish,* and *Tales of a Wayside Inn.*

On December 25, 1864, Longfellow composed his poem "Christmas Bells." It was a time of national suffering in America, and a time of personal melancholy for Longfellow. In 1861 he had lost his beloved wife, Fannie, in a tragic fire and had himself been severely burned while trying to extinguish the flames. He later wrote that the holidays were "inexpressibly sad," a sadness that deepened in 1863, when he received word that his son, Charles, a lieutenant with the Army of the Potomac, had been severely wounded in battle.

Consumed by grief for the nation's tragedies as well as his own, Longfellow heard the pealing of church bells on Christmas Day in 1864. He began to write, bitter words at first, until the bells, he said, began to lift his spirits. "Christmas Bells," set to music in 1872, became Longfellow's affirmation of the hope and mercy of the season.

> *I heard the bells on Christmas Day*
> *Their old familiar carols play,*
> *And wild and sweet*
> *The words repeat*
> *Of peace on earth, good-will to men!*

Like Longfellow, the Reverend Edmund Hamilton Sears was suffering personal melancholy when he composed "It Came upon the Midnight Clear" in 1849. Born in 1810 on a farm in the Berkshire Hills town of Sandisfield, Massachusetts, into a family that nurtured a love of poetry, Edmund Sears attended Union College in New York and later studied law. A fervent

Christmas Bells. Louis Prang postcard, c. 1885. Courtesy Boston Public Library Print Department.

abolitionist who had had moral duty impressed upon him by his parents, Sears was attracted to the writing and preaching of William Ellery Channing and in 1834 enrolled at Harvard Divinity School. Upon graduation, he served as a frontier missionary in Ohio. Offered a ministry in Wayland, Massachusetts, the shy and somewhat frail Sears accepted the position, attracted, he said, by the rural beauty and quiet of Wayland.

It was in his Wayland parsonage, by the fireside, on a cold, clear December evening, that Sears began his poem. Published in the *Christian Register,* "It Came upon the Midnight Clear" was criticized as being too humanistic, without enough piety and Scripture, but it reflected Sears's social and moral concerns as well as his independence as a thinker. The poem was set to music in 1850 by Richard Storrs Willis, a New York organist:

> *It came upon the midnight clear,*
> *That glorious song of old,*
> *From angels bending near the earth*
> *To touch their harps of gold;*
> *"Peace on the earth, good will to men,*
> *From heaven's all gracious King."*
> *The world in solemn stillness lay,*
> *To hear the angels sing.*

If the Reverend Sears's poem was thought not scriptural enough, the carol written by the Reverend John Henry Hopkins Jr., "We Three Kings," captured a scene right out of the Bible. Born in 1820 into an intellectual Pittsburgh family that nurtured a love of music, Hopkins was his father's namesake, the oldest son of eleven children. The elder Hopkins was already a successful lawyer when he was elected to fill a vacancy in his parish church. In 1832 he was elected the first Episcopal bishop of Vermont, serving until his death in 1868.

The Reverend John Henry Hopkins Jr.
Courtesy Diocese of Vermont.

The junior Hopkins, after graduating from the University of Vermont, worked as a reporter in New York and then enrolled in the General Theological Seminary in New York. He stayed on at the school after graduation to teach music and wrote the carol "We Three Kings" in 1857 as part of a Christmas pageant. Cherished world-wide, it is one of the few carols to relate the story of the Three Wise Men—and one of the few whose words and music were written by the same person.

> *We three kings of Orient are;*
> *Bearing gifts we traverse afar,*
> *Field and fountain, moor and mountain,*
> *Following yonder star.*
>
> *O star of wonder, star of light,*
> *Star with royal beauty bright,*
> *Westward leading, still proceeding,*
> *Guide us to thy perfect light.*

A Biblical event was also the inspiration for a carol written by the Reverend Phillips Brooks. With his keen intellect, charismatic personality, and oratorical gifts, Brooks electrified congregations as did few other preachers of the nineteenth century. When the Boston native and Harvard graduate returned to the city in 1869, after ten years of ministry at two Philadelphia churches, he became rector of Trinity Church, then a gloomy stone church in downtown Boston. By 1871 Trinity Church had purchased land in

Boston's newly filled Back Bay neighborhood, and ambitious plans were under way for a new sacred space to be designed in the Romanesque style by the architect Henry Hobson Richardson, who was Brooks's friend. Though the magnificent Trinity Church in Copley Square may be Brooks's most important legacy, he is best known as the author of "O Little Town of Bethlehem."

The Right Reverend Phillips Brooks, c. 1890. Courtesy Boston Public Library Print Department.

It was while serving in Philadelphia that Brooks was given the opportunity by parishioners to travel abroad, through the Holy Land, for a year. On Christmas Eve 1865, on a horseback pilgrimage from Jerusalem to Bethlehem, Brooks found himself in a peaceful field overlooking the little town. Later that evening he attended a Christmas Eve service, during which hymns resounded in the old church. Two years later Brooks reflected on the experience and put his thoughts into words, words that became "O Little Town of Bethlehem."

> *O little town of Bethlehem, how still we see thee lie!*
> *Above thy deep and dreamless sleep the silent stars go by.*
> *Yet in thy dark streets shineth the everlasting Light;*
> *The hopes and fears of all the years are met in thee tonight.*

If "Christmas Bells," "It Came upon the Midnight Clear," "We Three Kings," and "O Little Town of Bethlehem" were born of pious, thoughtful reflection, "Jingle Bells" was anything but. It is a bouncy song filled with frivolous fun and good cheer, despite its author having been the son of a Boston Unitarian pastor and prominent abolitionist.

James Lord Pierpont, born in Medford, Massachusetts, in 1822, was something of a rogue and a vagabond, abandoning his family to seek his fortune, first at sea and then in San Francisco during the Gold Rush. By 1853 the colorful Pierpont had followed his brother, the Reverend John Pierpont, to Savannah, Georgia, and had taken a position as music director at his brother's parish. There is some dispute as to whether Pierpont's song, originally issued as "One-Horse Open Sleigh," and later reissued as "Jingle

Bells," belongs to Medford or Savannah, Georgia. Both Medford and Savannah claim it as their own, and it may be that it was written while Pierpont was living in Medford and published after he moved to Savannah.

Sometimes described as a drag-racing song for the horse-and-buggy days, "Jingle Bells" is a merry little tune—never intended as a Christmas song—that drew on Pierpont's memories of boyhood New England winters, sleigh rides while at boarding school in New Hampshire, and cutter races between Medford and Malden. (A cutter was a type of light sleigh.)

Regardless of whether the cheery "Jingle Bells" belongs to Massachusetts or Georgia, it has become the most popular of the secular Christmas songs. For Savannah, where snow rarely falls, the song provides a little bit of New England winter:

> *Dashing thro' the snow*
> *In a one-horse open sleigh,*
> *O'er the fields we go,*
> *Laughing all the way;*
> *Bells on bob tail ring,*
> *Making spirits bright,*
> *Oh what sport to ride and sing*
> *A sleighing song tonight.*
>
> *Jingle bells, Jingle bells,*
> *Jingle all the way;*
> *Oh! what joy it is to ride*
> *In a one-horse open sleigh.*
> *Jingle bells, Jingle bells,*
> *Jingle all the way;*
> *Oh! what joy it is to ride*
> *In a one-horse open sleigh.*

Sleigh Bells Ring at Bevin Brothers Bells

IMAGINE CHRISTMAS without bells—and without one William Barton. In 1808 Barton was putting down roots in a small Connecticut town, Easthampton, founded only sixty-five years earlier by settlers from Eastham, Cape Cod. If the folks of Easthampton—later East Hampton—were hoping to live a quiet existence, all that changed when William Barton's innovative bell factory spawned an industry that earned the town the name "Jingle-town" and made it the bell-making capital of the world.

These days, the first thing one notices when one arrives in East Hampton is that folks take that legacy very seriously. All the street signs have a bell design, inscribed with "East Hampton—Bell Town," and as one drives around the village, there are other hints of a jingling past, including Barton Hill Road and a cluster of small byways named Bevin Boulevard, Bevin Road, Bevin Avenue, and Bevin Court—even a Bevin Pond—all named for the Bevin family who were early settlers of the East Hampton parish. By 1832 William Bevin, who learned the art of bell making from William Barton, had joined with his brother Chauncey and opened his own bell factory, Bevin Brothers. Two younger brothers, Abner and Philo, later joined the firm and in 1868 the company name was changed to Bevin Brothers Manufacturing Company. Today, at the end of Bevin Road is a sprawling redbrick factory that looks, at first glance, like an abandoned remnant from those early days. But then one hears the machinery, maybe even a bell, and realizes that at Bevin Brothers Manufacturing the past is forever present.

Like his great-great-grandfather Chauncey, Stan Bevin makes bells. He is the fifth generation of Bevins to make bells (a sixth generation is showing an interest, too), and all around him, in the building that dates from 1832, the ghosts of Stan's ancestors link him to a time in New England when sleigh bells jingled joyfully in winter wonderlands, when church bells called worshippers to Sunday service, fire bells rallied the bucket brigade, and door chimes welcomed a visitor. Stan says that his ancestors never thought of themselves as being simply bell makers. They were in the communication business, and if, as the legend says, God and the angels speak through bells,

It is my heart-warm and world-embracing Christmas hope and aspiration that all of us, the high, the low, the rich, the poor, the admired, the despised, the loved, the hated, the civilized, the savage (every man and brother of us all throughout the whole earth), may eventually be gathered together in a heaven of everlasting rest and peace and bliss, except the inventor of the telephone.   —Mark Twain, Christmas greeting, 1890

Bevin Brothers Manufacturing, c. 1900. Courtesy Connecticut Historical Society.

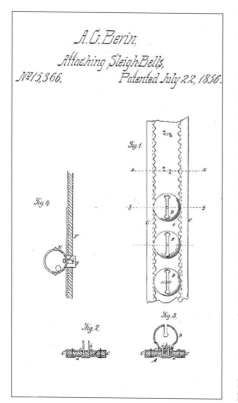

Bevin Bells patent, 1856. Courtesy United States Patent and Trademark Office.

then Bevin Brothers surely was, and is, doing godly work.

William Bevin learned well as an indentured servant to William Barton, and when he and Chauncey opened their factory doors in 1832, their specialty was sleigh bells, core cast in the same way that Barton had first cast them, in one piece rather than in two halves that were soldered together. The process was imperfect and the bells were imperfect, but that was what gave them their unique, mellow musicality. So distinct was each set of bells that it was said that one could tell who was coming by the jingle.

If today the old sleigh bells are a nostalgic, decorative touch to the mo-

The Bells

Hear the sledges with the bells,
Silver bells!
What a world of merriment their melody foretells!
How they tinkle, tinkle, tinkle,
In the icy air of night!
While the stars that oversprinkle
All the heavens seem to twinkle
With a crystalline delight;
Keeping time, time, time,
In a sort of Runic rhyme,
To the tintinnabulation that so musically wells
From the bells, bells, bells, bells,
Bells, bells, bells—
From the jingling and the tinkling of the bells.

—Edgar Allen Poe

dern holiday, they were in Bevin's day purely functional. Mandated by law, bells were used on horses to warn pedestrians of a swiftly approaching sleigh, otherwise silent in the deep quiet of a snow-covered winter road. Besides sleigh bells, the brothers also manufactured cow and sheep bells and ships' bells, all now simple relics of a bygone New England.

Today, though its musical product has diversified to meet the changing needs of a changing society, Bevin Brothers still makes only bells, the sole American company to do so. And though there may not be the demand for sleigh bells that there once was in William and Chauncey Bevin's day, there is one sleigh—pulled by eight reindeer—that returns every year to Bevin Brothers to have its bells polished and repaired.

Imagine Christmas without bells.

God Bless Us, Every One!

IT WAS DURING Boston's "golden age" of literature—when Harvard College, the Boston Public Library, and the Boston Athenaeum housed

America's most important literary collections, when Longfellow, Haw-thorne, Holmes, Emerson, and Whittier, among others, met monthly at the Saturday Club at the Parker House, and when William Ticknor and James Fields were preeminent American publishers—that the distinguished English writer Charles Dickens paid a second visit to the city.

In 1842, as a young man of thirty, the newly famous Dickens had visited Boston for the first time while on an American tour. He was embraced warmly, made many new friends, and noted, with fondness, that Boston reminded him of London. A quarter century passed before Dickens again stepped ashore in America, and when he arrived in Boston on November 19, 1867, for a five-month reading tour, his reputation was mythological. He had become literary royalty.

Despite his precarious health during the visit, Dickens maintained a busy and full schedule of walks, luncheons, dinners, sightseeing, and readings. He took up residence at the splendid Parker House—"Parker's"—opened by Harvey Parker in 1856 at the corner of Tremont and School Streets and, as he had during his first visit, attracted crowds of admirers wherever he went. But what Bostonians most eagerly awaited were his readings, especially his readings from *A Christmas Carol.*

Published in 1843, after his previous visit to America, *A Christmas Carol* was the story of the miserly Ebenezer Scrooge, the long-suffering Bob Cratchit, and his dying son, Tiny Tim. It was Dickens's first Christmas story, written in six weeks and published at a time when England's industrial revolution and the demand on workers to increase productivity left little time for Christmas joy. Dickens himself was despairing about the plight of the poor and working class.

Feuding with his publishers at the time, Dickens self-published the book, paying for gilt edging, lavish binding, and illustrations by John Leech. Hoping to rekindle the spirit of Christmas, he priced the book at five shillings so that it would be affordable for most readers. Despite the book's being an instant success, its high production costs left little profit for its author.

The story's scenes of blissful family life, holiday revelry, plum pudding, and presents belied Dickens's anguish, but it spurred a Christmas revival in England. In New England, where Christmas had long been suppressed, it finally began to be embraced. In fact, so closely was Dickens associated with Christmas that many Americans believed he had *invented* Christmas!

Illustration by John Leech for *A Christmas Carol,* 1843.
Courtesy Dover Publications.

Tremont Temple, 1858. Courtesy Boston Athenaeum.

The first Bostonians to hear *A Christmas Carol* were the members of the Saturday Club, which had been founded in 1855, who had a private reading on November 30, 1867. Two nights later Dickens debuted at the Tremont Temple, just steps from the Parker House. Always with a flair for the dramatic—he had performed regularly in amateur theatricals—Dickens relished the opportunity to read in front of audiences. But he did much more than simply read: he performed. He strode onto the stage, a stage empty of props, and filled it with individual characters' voices, with animation, stamina, enthusiasm, with all the wretchedness of the society whose wrongs he was hoping to expose. One observer called him a "human hurricane." So nuanced and real were his characterizations that it was said that the scene in which Tiny Tim dies had audiences sobbing into their handkerchiefs.

Dickens repeated his reading of *A Christmas Carol* on Christmas Eve, again to a delighted and enthusiastic audience. He gave seventy-six performances during his tour of East Coast cities, including his last American reading in Boston, on April 8, 1868, before setting sail for England. Two years later he died, at the age of fifty-eight.

In the years since, *A Christmas Carol* has become a beloved holiday favorite, retold in countless book editions, film versions, and theatrical productions. In its sympathetic treatment of the poor, the suffering, and the oppressed, and in its potent message that we are all one, that ignorance and want are everyone's children, *A Christmas Carol* speaks to the true meaning of Christmas: that through the spirit of goodwill and generosity we can all be reborn.

Portrait of Charles Dickens, 1867.
Courtesy Boston Athenaeum.

(It is in this spirit that Boston University's public radio station, WBUR-FM, gives an annual reading of *A Christmas Carol* to benefit Rosie's Place, a shelter for homeless women and their children in Boston.)

Ode to Christmas

For a certain generation of Bostonians, the Emmy and Peabody Award–winning reporter and commentator Chuck Kraemer is fondly remembered for his insightful writing and dry wit. When families sat down to dinner, so often in front of the local newscast, there he was, for twenty years at Channel 5, for another five at Channel 2. And he always seemed to be having fun.

In 1976 he wrote a quirky little tongue-twisting ditty called "Ode to Christmas" to end one of the newscasts during Christmas week. He dashed it off, he says, and had no inkling at the time that it would make any kind of an impression with viewers. But it did. The following year he tweaked it a bit, to bring it up to date, and performed it again at the end of the newscast, much to the delight of Channel 5 viewers.

Year after year, whether it aired on Channel 5, Channel 2, or National Public Radio, "Ode to Christmas" became Chuck Kraemer's gift to us all. We

chuckled at its cleverness, we were amazed that he could recite it all so lightning fast and flawlessly (he says it never took more than two or three takes),
and when it was over, in a minute and a half, we yearned to hear it again.
But, like Christmas, it came but once a year, and that's what made it so
delicious.

Underlying the lightness of the verse was something a little darker, a cynicism about the modern Christmas and its commercialism that tapped into
uneasy feelings many folks were having about the holiday. We knew we
could not stop the commercial juggernaut that we had created, but "Ode to
Christmas" let us laugh at ourselves and it made us stop, for ninety seconds
at least, to consider what, indeed, we had done to Christmas.

And so, here is Chuck's last "Ode," from Christmas 2003. It was not
meant to be read, but heard in Chuck's lilting, soothing voice with em-
phases in all the right places. Still, for Bostonians of a certain age, even the
words on paper will sing, as they always did.

> Lord . . . & Taylor. Ann Taylor. Ann & Hope. Anne Klein, Calvin Klein,
> Cuisinart, Kodak, cotton polyester, budget stretcher, store-wide, half off,
> cashmere, dot-com.
>
> Foosball.
>
> Flat-panel, classic flannel, multi-channel, joystick, rain check, Osh-
> Kosh, goose down, Smack Down, Snoop Dogg.
>
> Old Navy, New Balance, Joe Boxer, Big Bertha, Bugle Boy, Game Boy,
> Spiderman, Mr. Coffee, Fry Daddy, Dirt Devil, Dolby, Barbie, Fuji,
> khaki, karaoke, Yahtzee, Sorry.
>
> Toll-free, hands-free, earbuds, ab toner, Foot Locker, famous maker,
> subwoofer, Tweeter, Starter, Russell Stover, Eddie Bauer, Perry Ellis,
> Harry Potter, Laura Ashley, Circuit City, Sam Goody, Abercrombie,
> Fanny Farmer, Scooby Doo.
>
> Behold in the east, a star . . . bucks, brushed aluminum, travel mug,
> a divine . . . Miss M, mini CD, Kenny G, HD, HP, dpi, LCD, JVC, DVD,
> GE, GI Joe, IJ Fox, TJ Maxx, fax, Pentax, FedEx, AmEx, Gore-Tex,
> Timex, Reebok, e-Bay, O-lympus, Ar-mani, J. Crew, I-bu . . . profen.
>
> Givenchy, Jontue, Jean Naté, Cachet, Fabergé, automatic layaway.
>
> Norelco, Casio, Polo, Lego, Toro, Osco, Speedo, Nemo, Hasbro,
> Tyco, Tonka, Martha, Sherpa, Ninja, Plasma, Duracell, Duraflame, Lon-
> don Fog, Swiss Army, Canadian Club, Scotch tape, English Leather,
> Irish Mist, British Sterling, Sterling Silver, Lady Schick, sure-stick, non-
> stick, Water-Pik, Shreve, Crump, Low, watt, crock, pot.
>
> One-touch, U2, MP3, four slice, 5 x 7, 1-800, nine-volt, ten-speed,

12-cup, 19-inch, kilo, mega, giga, tera, byte, white sale, infra-red, Wal-greens, Black & Decker, what the heck . . . deck the halls with Hitachi, Mitsubishi, Sansui, Sony, Seiko, Sanyo, Panasonic, Instamatic, anti-static, alkaline, nine to nine, Calvin Klein, Anne Klein, Ann & Hope, Ann Taylor, Lord & Taylor, good Lord.

What have we done to Christmas?

Dylan Thomas and the Dean

HE WAS KNOWN as the Dean of Talk Radio, and for years Jerry Williams ruled the Boston airwaves during drive time, 3:00–7:00 P.M. Listeners either loved him or hated him, but no one could deny that he turned talk radio into an agent for change. Like another acerbic commentator on the political scene, the nineteenth-century cartoonist Thomas Nast, Williams kept politicians under a microscope and used his bully pulpit to expose waste and corruption.

He opened every program with a cheery "Hello, New England" and was famous for a handful of one-liners—"I'm getting out of the business," "He's not a bad guy," and "I never had a dinner"—that he tossed off, with impec-cable timing, at just the right moment to break the tension. He espoused populist ideals and championed the little guy, spearheading campaigns against tax hikes and bureaucracy, the mandatory seat belt law, the Big Dig, and the construction of a prison in the tiny Massachusetts town of New Braintree.

But, like Thomas Nast, who also delighted readers of *Harper's Weekly* with his enchanting Christmas illustrations, Jerry Williams too had a softer side. He loved antiques and music, and every December, a week or two before Christmas, he'd dedicate the better part of a program to the reading of Dylan Thomas's *A Child's Christmas in Wales*. It was Williams's Christmas gift to his loyal listeners and to any-one else who might be spinning the dial and have the good fortune to land on AM 680. He'd announce the particular day ahead of time so that his regulars could settle in with a cup of cider or hot chocolate; politicians and

Jerry Williams. Courtesy Museum of Broadcast Communications/ Radio Hall of Fame.

government workers would breathe a sigh of relief that for one afternoon, at least, they would be spared his wrath.

Published posthumously in 1955, though Thomas read and recorded the story before his death in 1953, *A Child's Christmas in Wales* was Dylan Thomas's affectionate look back at the fondest Christmas memories of his childhood—the uncles, the useful and useless presents, the "gravy smell" of dinners, the music, the cats, and the crocheted nose bags—all garlanded together into one perfect Christmas. The anecdotes recall the sensuous pleasures of Christmas, the magic of childhood, family gatherings, and newly fallen snow; their overall effect was to evoke pure nostalgia for an old-fashioned Christmas that all hoped might be theirs.

Thomas, who had always been fascinated by radio, wrote the story as a radio script. The effect of hearing the musical passages and letting one's own imagination create the scene may explain why the readings so captivated Jerry Williams's audiences year after year:

> One Christmas was so much like another, in those years around the sea-town corner now and out of all sound except the distant speaking of the voices I sometimes hear a moment before sleep, that I can never remember whether it snowed for six days and six nights when I was twelve or whether it snowed for twelve days and twelve nights when I was six. All the Christmases roll down toward the two-tongued sea, like a cold and headlong moon bundling down the sky that was our street; and they stop at the rim of the ice-edged, fish-freezing waves, and I plunge my hands in the snow and bring out whatever I can find.

A Beacon Hill Christmas

IT IS OFTEN SAID that one person can inspire the world, and it just may be that a lad by the name of Alfred Shurtleff was that one person, the sole inspiration, at least in New England, for the widespread use of the decorative window light, one of the most elegant expressions of the Christmas season, a tradition first brought to America by Irish immigrants who placed a candle in the window on Christmas Eve to welcome the parish priest for midnight Mass.

As the story was told in a 1929 Boston newspaper article, back in 1893, on Christmas Eve, young Shurtleff had placed a single candle in the bedroom window of his 9 West Cedar Street home on Beacon Hill. There was no objection by neighbors to the display; indeed, several were inspired to light their own candles. The following year, others in the neighborhood joined in and it seemed that Alfred had begun a new tradition.

In 1898, with his parents away in Europe, Alfred Shurtleff got adventurous and placed half a dozen candles in windows. Though the display was again greeted with enthusiasm by neighbors and passersby, the neighborhood tradition waned. Within a few years, only the Shurtleffs were lighting up for the holiday.

But on Christmas Eve in 1907, Mr. and Mrs. Ralph Adams Cram—he was the architect of the Church of the Advent at Mt. Vernon and Brimmer Streets—were sitting by the fire with friends, wishing for lights—perhaps recalling the beautiful effect of the white lights of a decade earlier—and music. Spontaneously, they went outdoors and began to sing carols in the silent streets.

The next year, on December 23, the Crams' Beacon Hill neighbors received an invitation, written in Old English script:

> In order to promote a spirit of good will and Christmas cheer the undersigned request that you contribute to that end by placing lighted candles in the windows of your house fronting on the street between the hours of seven and ten o'clock of Christmas Eve.
>
> Mr. and Mrs. Ralph Adams Cram
> Mr. and Mrs. Arthur Winslow
> Mr. and Mrs. Hollis French
> Mr. and Mrs. Roger Warner
> The Chestnut Street Christmas Association.

A Beacon Hill neighbor, Mr. Clarence Hillsmith, replied to the invitation in his own Old English script:

> We habitants of Six Acorn Street on ye hillside hasten in reply of ye yuletide herald. On ye eve before Day of Glad Tidings will be illumined this habitation. Candles will light on their way whomsoever passeth over ye cobbles.
> May happiness attend them.

Word of the event spread and even those residents of Beacon Hill who had not received an invitation joined in the spirit of goodwill and placed candles in their windows. The following year a reminder was sent by the

Chestnut Street Christmas Association announcing that windows would again be ablaze:

> To All Whom it May Concern
>   Greeting! We again bespeak your good will and assistance in adding to the cheer of Christmas Eve by placing lighted candles in the windows of your house between 6 and 10 at night, to the end that the hearts of passersby may be gladdened and that the day of good will and glad tidings may be fittingly commemorated.

Carolers also came to Beacon Hill that Christmas Eve, muffled in coats, hats, and scarves and carrying Japanese lanterns. Other carolers came at dawn. One tradition had been revived and a new one begun.

If there was any neighborhood that was the perfect backdrop for Christmas candlelight and caroling in the tradition of the old English waits—village carolers—it was Beacon Hill, a cozy, nineteenth-century enclave with redbrick sidewalks, narrow cobblestone streets, wrought-iron fences, gas street lamps, and purple-paned windows. By the mid-1920s, not only had caroling and window lights firmly established themselves as a necessary part of the Christmas season, but a new Christmas Eve tradition had begun on Beacon Hill—handbell ringing.

If there was some debate as to when and how the candle lighting had begun, there was no question that Mrs. Margaret Shurcliff had brought bells to Beacon Hill. Before her marriage in 1905 to Arthur Shurcliff, the brother of Alfred Shurtleff (Arthur changed the spelling of his surname in 1930 to conform to the Old English), the young Margaret had accompanied her father, Arthur Nichols, a prominent Boston physician and tower bell ringer at Old North Church in Boston, to England in 1902 to learn bell ringing. At a time when only men rang bells, Margaret became the first American woman to ring a complete peal on tower bells in England. Her English hosts presented her with a set of eight Whitechapel handbells, and over the years Margaret expanded her bell collection and introduced friends and family to the joys of ringing. In 1924 Margaret began the tradition of bell ringing on Christmas Eve on Beacon Hill. Her Beacon Hill Bell Ringers included five of her six children and several friends.

In 1937 several bell-ringing enthusiasts met at Margaret's home and formed the New England Guild of English Handbell Ringers. Margaret, who served as the guild's first president, was described in the guild's journal

Mrs. Arthur Shurcliff (*left*) and bell ringers on Beacon Hill, 1958.
Courtesy Boston Public Library Print Department.

as "tall and stately and friendly. She is a charming hostess, a fascinating story teller, has a delightful sense of humor, and is devoted to the art of handbell ringing."

As interest in handbell ringing spread, the American Guild of English Handbell Ringers was formed in 1954, and the first handbell festival was held at the Crane mansion in Ipswich, Massachusetts.

Margaret Shurcliff passed away in 1959, but the Myrer family continued the tradition of bell ringing on Christmas Eve until the early 1970s, when it began to wane. It was then that Mary Jane Sawyer, joined by Arthur Shurcliff, Margaret's grandson, stepped in and kept the tradition alive.

Today the bells ring out every Christmas Eve from Louisburg Square, where the homeowners' association coordinates the event. Each year a family hosts the bell ringers, who perform—no matter what the weather—traditional carols for the thousands who stroll Beacon Hill during the evening.

I'll Be Home for Christmas

Born in 1873, Bernice James was a girl from Hull, a tiny seaside community in Massachusetts. She was said to have been a woman of plain tastes whose passion had always been music. An accomplished pianist, she studied opera in Milan and made her operatic debut in 1900. She married the Italian tenor Salvatore de Pasquali, who formed his own opera troupe with Bernice as principal soprano. On January 2, 1909, the "bird-voiced singer" made her Metropolitan Opera debut as Violetta in *La Traviata*. Madame de Pasquali electrified her audience and was called out for twenty-six

Bernice James de Pasquali, c. 1910.
Courtesy Metropolitan Opera Archives.

curtain calls. She remained at the Met as principal coloratura soprano for six years, singing fifty-six performances. Few sopranos of the day could rival Bernice's fifty-four-opera repertoire.

If you could take the girl out of Hull, there was no taking Hull out of the girl. An international star who had sung with Caruso and been conducted by Gustav Mahler, Bernice James de Pasquali remained a small-town girl to the end. When she wasn't performing at Christmastime she came home to share the holiday, gathering family and friends in Elm Square, in front of the library, to sing "Silent Night" on Christmas Eve.

In 1925 Bernice James de Pasquali came home one last time and was laid to rest in the village cemetery next to her beloved husband, Salvatore, who had died two years earlier.

A Norman Rockwell Christmas

IF THERE WAS ANY American artist who conveyed the nobility of familiar, everyday life, embraced the idealism of the American spirit, and showed the American people themselves, it was the illustrator Norman Rockwell.

A New Yorker by birth, Rockwell moved his family in 1939 to Vermont, where he began painting the story of small-town American life. For nearly half a century his portrayals of families and pets, station wagons and ballgames, graced the covers of the *Saturday Evening Post,* the magazine that Rockwell said was the "greatest show window in America."

By 1953 the Rockwell family—his wife, Mary, and their three sons, Jarvis, Thomas, and Peter—had settled in Stockbridge, Massachusetts, a peaceful village, once an Indian mission, in the Berkshire Hills. There family, friends, and neighbors gladly dressed in historical costumes, held props, and lent their faces and figures to Rockwell's scenes. Rockwell, a stickler for technique, detail, and accuracy, had a knack for finding just the right face for his subjects. He later said that there were few folks in the village who, at one time or another, hadn't modeled for him.

In December 1916 Rockwell illustrated his first Christmas cover, "Playing Santa," for the weekly *Saturday Evening Post.* Three years passed before Rockwell did another Christmas cover, but then, for the next three decades, a Norman Rockwell illustration graced a December cover and became as familiar a tradition as picking out a tree or hanging a wreath. Even after Rockwell's departure from the *Saturday Evening Post,* his Christmas illustrations, and the stories they told, continued to enchant. Hallmark cards issued an immensely popular line of Rockwell Christmas cards during the 1940s and 1950s, and Brown and Bigelow, specializing in advertising and promotional materials, engaged his services for an equally popular series of calendars.

In 1956 Rockwell was approached by the editors of *McCall's* magazine to illustrate the magazine's December 1957 cover. The artist looked no farther than his own beloved Stockbridge for inspiration, but his busy schedule kept him from completing the painting until December 1967. Though the painting's landscape theme was a departure from his usual perceptive and witty illustrations depicting human relationships, Rockwell's panoramic view of the village, *Stockbridge at Christmas,* gave his audience a heartwarming scene of quaint downtown shops and buildings garlanded in greens and colored lights, shoppers bustling to and fro, and children playing in the snow.

It became the quintessential expression of small-town New England life—and an old-fashioned Christmas.

Today, decades later, Stockbridge, home to the Norman Rockwell Museum, still looks much as it did when Rockwell called it "the best of America, the best of New England." Every December the local Chamber of Commerce re-creates Rockwell's magical Main Street scene, complete with vintage cars. Visitors who take in the scene are reminded not only of yesteryear, but also of the timelessness of Christmas and its enduring message of fellowship and goodwill.

Welcome Yule: The Revels

BACK IN DECEMBER 1957, when the late John Langstaff debuted his Revels in New York, even he could not have imagined the place that his unique, indeed radical, new theatrical experience—a celebratory program of pre-Christian ritual and folk music and medieval English revelry that invited audience participation—would eventually earn in the hearts of holiday theatergoers. That New York debut, though critically acclaimed, did not win the Revels overnight success, and throughout the 1960s Langstaff fine-tuned his program and incorporated many of its elements into other theatrical productions.

In 1971 Langstaff and his daughter, Carol, brought the Revels to Sanders Theatre at Harvard University in Cambridge, Massachusetts, for two performances. It was a modest beginning, but what began simply as a way for Langstaff to share his favorite medieval English music and dance in time became a cherished Christmas tradition that has brought more than a million people joyously together to share the winter solstice.

Being born on Christmas Eve may have presaged the future for John Langstaff. He grew up in a Brooklyn Heights brownstone that his Anglophile parents and their Anglophile friends filled with traditional music, dance, mummers' plays, and storytelling. Each year, on Christmas Eve, the caroling "waits" of the neighborhood gathered at the Langstaff home to begin their procession through the Heights. By the age of eight, Langstaff had entered the Grace Church Choir School in New York City; he later received classical training at Juilliard and Curtis. After a successful international career as a concert baritone, he came full circle, back to the traditional music and dance of his childhood.

John Langstaff and the Revels company. Courtesy Revels, Inc., Watertown, Massachusetts.

With the Christmas Revels, Langstaff set out to explore the ways that ancient peoples across diverse cultures connected with the natural world and shared and celebrated the midwinter season. Langstaff believed that the old myths and rituals still had meaning and relevance for modern audiences. From the beginning, at the heart of the Christmas Revels was the bringing together of people. Just as ancient peoples, young and old, had joined together to sing, dance, and drive the dark away on the longest night of the year, so too did young and old, professional and amateur, join together on the Revels stage. Audience members, too, joined together in a "temporary community," united in song and dance by the powerful effects of myth, music, and ritual.

For his early productions, Langstaff drew inspiration from the familiar medieval English traditions of his childhood, but in time the Christmas Revels began traveling around the world, incorporating traditions from diverse cultures—from Appalachia to Russia, from Italy to French Canada. Always, though, the Revels kept one foot firmly planted in English tradition. Over the years several pieces, particularly Susan Cooper's evocative poem "The Shortest Day," "The Sussex Mummers' Carol," and Sydney Carter's "The

Lord of the Dance," the joyful dance that symbolizes the life force of the winter solstice and of the Revels, became signature pieces that audiences expected at every performance. On one occasion, when for historical accuracy "The Lord of the Dance" was not included in the program, the audience took it upon themselves to join hands spontaneously and sing it anyway. It may be that at that moment, John Langstaff's dream of bringing people together in a joyful, communal celebration had been realized.

If, over the decades, the content of Revels performances has broadened—though every six or seven years the Revels "comes home" to Tudor England—its mission of celebrating the seasons and the cycles of life, honoring the ties that bind cultures during the midwinter season, and cultivating an understanding of traditional dance, drama, and ritual has stayed constant, true to Langstaff's original vision. Historical accuracy, though important to the Revels' production staff, is not as important, they say, as nourishing the human spirit, encouraging fellowship and peace, and sharing the hopefulness of the season.

Now a national, year-round organization, the Revels has production companies in ten cities and towns. The Christmas Revels remains the mighty trunk of the oak, but its branches have spread out to bring audiences exuberant celebrations of midsummer, the harvest, and the sea. Each reminds us of our beginnings and our shared traditions, but the Christmas Revels especially reminds us that even on the darkest night, there is something to sing about.

A Peter Hunt Christmas

WHEN THE FOLK ARTIST Peter Hunt first came to Provincetown, Massachusetts, at the tip of Cape Cod in the early 1920s, he found a "little village of workers." People made what they needed, he noted, "soap, hooked rugs, jams, jellies, quilts, curious carvings, inlaid tables." The happiest people he knew, he said, were "those who make things with their hands, either as a recreation or professionally."

Hunt would be one of those people who made things with their hands, decorating old pieces of cast-off furniture and household items with bold, bright colors and whimsical "peasant" designs of angels, flowers, and horses, transforming ordinary items into works of art. To the peasant at heart, wrote Hunt:

One of Peter Hunt's Christmas designs. Courtesy Lynn Van Dine/The Search for Peter Hunt.

Christmas is a heyday—the best time of the year to make things for:
nothing is too small, nothing too large, nothing impossible. Old customs are revived, new ones originated. Old songs must be sung, new
ones written. Old friends must be greeted—the new ones, too. Everything must be stopped so a note or a beautiful card or a happy present
can be sent to every friend who is away from you. Plain paper isn't
worthy on this day—it must be bright and glittering. Christmas is indeed a wonderful time.

In his Christmas shop in the seaside village of Provincetown, where Portuguese fishermen trimmed their trees "entirely with strings of shells from
the beaches," Hunt created his own happy and glittering version of a warm,
peaceful, merry Christmas, a Christmas filled with stars and snowflakes, hollies and mistletoes, sleighs, angels, pine trees, gingerbread boys and girls,
candy canes, and plum puddings—all interpreted in his imaginative style.

On a Sleigh Ride with the Boston Pops

BACK IN FEBRUARY 1948, when Leroy Anderson took his newest orches-
tral piece to the legendary Boston Pops conductor, Arthur Fiedler, he
could not have imagined that "Sleigh Ride" would become one of the Pops'
all-time classics, indeed, many would argue, its signature piece. Few who
find themselves spontaneously caught up in the song's buoyant Christmas
joy and its sparkling "picture" of a winter wonderland know that "Sleigh
Ride" was not written specifically as a Christmas piece and was composed on
a sweltering hot July day, in Connecticut, in the midst of a New England
heat wave.

Beginning in the 1930s, the Boston-born Arthur Fiedler, who had joined
the Boston Symphony Orchestra in 1915 and become the first American
conductor of the Pops in 1930, and Leroy Anderson, the Harvard-educated
son of Swedish immigrants who had mastered eight languages and intended
to become a language teacher, began a long and close musical relationship
that lasted nearly forty years. In 1936 Anderson composed the first of many
light classical pieces for the Boston Pops Orchestra, founded in 1885 as a
"popular" alternative to the esteemed Boston Symphony Orchestra. Until
his death in 1975, the prolific Anderson would compose for the Pops;
decades later his music remains integral to the life of the orchestra.

"Sleigh Ride" was first performed, probably as an encore, by the Boston
Pops, with Arthur Fiedler conducting, on May 4, 1948. The Pops recorded

Arthur Fiedler. Photo by Jet, courtesy Boston Pops Orchestra.

Leroy Anderson. Courtesy
Anderson family and
www.Leroy-Anderson.com.

The first page of the sheet music for "Sleigh Ride." Music by Leroy Anderson/words by Mitchell Parish. © 1948, 1950 (renewed) EMI MILLS MUSIC Inc. All rights reserved.

"Sleigh Ride" in April 1949, and in 1950 Mitchell Parrish added lyrics. Said to have been "pleasantly received" by Pops audiences, "Sleigh Ride"—and Leroy Anderson—would in time establish itself in the hearts of audiences everywhere. No other American composer's works would be performed more by American orchestras than Anderson's.

In 1974, only months after celebrating Independence Day with the first spectacular Fourth of July concert and fireworks on Boston's Esplanade, Arthur Fiedler launched A Pops Christmas Party—later known as Holiday Pops—with a three-concert series. "Sleigh Ride," with its creative instrumental effects—its sleigh bells and whinnying horse, its whip crack and clip-clop cadence of hoofbeats—magically captured the essence and ageless rhythms of the holiday season and became the treasured highlight of the Boston Pops Christmas repertoire, sometimes performed as an encore, sometimes in the program, but *always* performed. So closely identified with Holiday Pops had Anderson's composition become over the years that when Keith Lockhart (the current conductor) and the Boston Pops Orchestra released its first-ever self-produced, self-distributed CD in 2005, they named it, appropriately, *Sleigh Ride.*

Today around New England, where Christmas music is synonymous with the Boston Pops, Holiday Pops—now with children's matinees, holiday treats, and visits with Santa—is a cherished family tradition. Beginning the second week of December and continuing through New Year's Eve, the Pops performs nearly forty concerts at a festively decorated Symphony Hall, with additional concerts performed around New England. There's something for everyone and every taste: chorals, medleys, and sing-a-longs, celebrity readings of *A Visit from St. Nicholas* and *How the Grinch Stole Christmas,* the "Hallelujah" chorus from Handel's *Messiah,* folk carols and *The Nutcracker,* "White Christmas" and "Frosty."

For a certain generation of music lovers, the ring-ting-tingling and giddy-yap, giddy-yap of Anderson's "Sleigh Ride" evoke not only Christmas cheer and the winter season, but also the fondest memories of childhood Christmases. For them, Christmas isn't Christmas without "Sleigh Ride." Christmas programs worldwide perform "Sleigh Ride," often compared in its charming nostalgia to Norman Rockwell's paintings, and singers and musicians from André Rieu, Johnny Mathis, and Dolly Parton to Ella Fitzgerald, the Canadian Brass, the New York Philharmonic, and even the Dixie Chicks have recorded the piece.

The cover of the sheet music for "Sleigh Ride." Music by Leroy Anderson/words by Mitchell Parish. © 1948, 1950 (renewed) EMI MILLS MUSIC Inc. All rights reserved.

It may be that the lyricist Mitchell Parrish said it best when he wrote, "These wonderful things are the things we remember/All through our lives." Indeed, whether it is Anderson's "Sleigh Ride" or the Holiday Pops, both have become an uplifting, enduring, indelible part of Christmas in New England.

A young girl named Ada Louise Taylor on a sled, c. 1890.
Courtesy Connecticut Historical Society.

VII. Let It Snow

F OR NEW ENGLANDERS, Christmas is extra special if a little bit of the white stuff falls on cue. Even folks living in warmer climates associate Christmas with the cold and the snow, an ancestral memory, perhaps, of pagan midwinter festivals in Northern Europe.

There seemed always to be snow (even if there wasn't), deep, seamless snow, for the Christmases of childhood. Its fragile beauty blanketed and veiled backyards and neighborhoods. Swirled by the winds, snow was piled

A Snow Scene on Boston Common. From *Ballou's Pictorial Drawingroom Companion,* 1856. Courtesy Dover Publications.

123

Young boy with a sled, c. 1940. Courtesy Bostonian Society/Old State House/
Arthur Hansen Photograph Collection.

high into drifts. Tree branches seemed to drip with icing. Everything that
had been familiar and mundane was new and exciting after a snowstorm.
The world outside had been remade.

For New Englanders, the probability that snow would fall sometime before spring arrived meant that certain presents were invariably under the
tree and in stockings on Christmas morning. There were mittens and muffs,
sweaters, scarves, and snowsuits, sleds, saucers, toboggans, and any other
contraption that could propel one down a hill. There might also be skates, a
scraper for the car windows, a new shovel.

And no matter how thrilled we were that Santa had remembered to bring
the special toy or game or doll, not one of those long-awaited, much-anticipated, had-to-have gifts seemed to matter if there was snow on the ground.
Snow was its own special gift. You'd stand there in the cold, in a hypnotic
trance, watching flakes fall, trying to catch one on an outstretched tongue.
You'd risk life and limb to break a shimmering icicle off the gutter. You'd
pass hours, indeed whole afternoons, playing and building in the blue-
shadowed backyard, creating snowmen, igloos, and forts (and stocking

those forts with arsenals of snowballs), and tracing angels in the untouched corners of the yard.

Snowflake Bentley

MUCH OF WHAT we know about snowflakes we owe to a passionate, curious Vermont farmer, Wilson Bentley, whom the world has come to know as "Snowflake" Bentley, and if ever there was a man who loved winter, it was he.

Born in 1865 on a farm in Jericho, he was from an early age fascinated by all forms of precipitation, but especially snow, which he examined under an old microscope his mother had given him. Frustrated that only he could enjoy the exquisite, evanescent beauty of each flake, Wilson tried drawing the intricate designs. But no sooner had he trained his lens on the crystal and begun the painstaking drawing, than it was gone, melted away. If only, he thought, he could capture the beauty of snowflakes and share them with the world.

Wilson "Snowflake" Bentley. Courtesy Wilson Bentley Digital Archives/Jericho Historical Society, www.snowflakebentley.com.

Make a Paper Snowflake

WHAT YOU WILL NEED: Small plates or round templates in various sizes (not too small, or cutting will be difficult); sheets of thin white paper or tissue paper; pencil; scissors; glue and glitter (optional)

How to make your snowflake:

1. Lay plate or template on the paper and trace.
2. Cut out the circle and fold it in half. Divide the half circle in thirds and fold. Your folded paper will look like a pizza wedge.
3. Fold the wedge in half and draw designs on the three edges. Cut out designs (you can also cut freehand, without drawing a design first).
4. Unfold the paper to see your snowflake. Daub with glue and decorate with glitter, if desired.

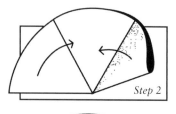

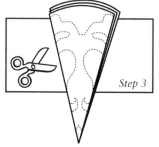

Two of Bentley's snowflakes. Courtesy Wilson Bentley Digital Archives/Jericho Historical Society, www.snowflakebentley.com.

Very little evidence of God or man did I see just then, and life not as rich and inviting an enterprise as it should be, when my attention was caught by a snowflake on my coat-sleeve. It was one of those perfect, crystalline, star-shaped ones, six-rayed, like a flat wheel with six spokes, only the spokes were perfect little pine trees in shape, arranged around a central spangle. This little object, which, with many of its fellows, rested unmelting on my coat, so perfect and beautiful, reminded me that Nature had not lost her pristine vigor yet, and why should man lose heart?

Henry David Thoreau, Journal, 1858

When Wilson was seventeen, his parents gave him a camera equipped with a microscope. Working enthusiastically through every snowstorm in an open-air woodshed, he taught himself how to photograph and capture the fragile, transient beauty of snowflakes. It would become his life's work, and his thousands upon thousands of images led him to conclude that no two snowflakes were alike. In 1931 more than two thousand of Bentley's photomicrographs on glass lantern slides, made over a span of fifty years, were collected in a book, *Snow Crystals*.

Snowflake Bentley lived just long enough to see his life's work published. Less than a month after the book's debut, Wilson caught pneumonia walking home in a snowstorm. Two weeks later, he died. But his book, a tribute to his skill, his patience, his curiosity, and his aesthetic appreciation for the tiny, fragile flakes, became his gift to the world.

Chester Greenwood and His Earmuffs

EARMUFFS: their mere mention provokes a chuckle, and chuckle the children did back in the winter of 1873, when their friend Chester Greenwood of Farmington, Maine, no longer able to bear the bitter cold days of Maine's winters, fashioned loops from farm wire and, with his grandmother's sewing skills, padded them with beaver fur and black velvet. He called his device an ear-muffler and until then, no one had heard of such a thing. The only way to keep the ears warm was to wrap one's head in a thick, bulky, itchy wool scarf.

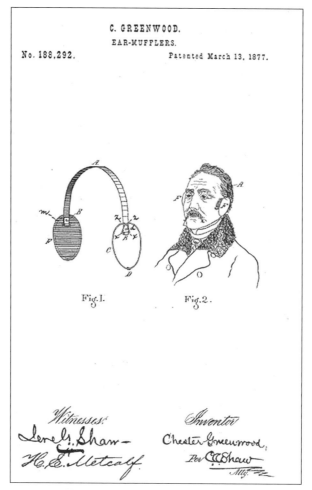

Chester Greenwood's ear-muffler patent.
Courtesy United States Patent and Trademark Office.

Born December 4, 1858, to Zina and Emily Greenwood, young Chester, though a grammar school dropout, was destined to succeed in business. By twelve he was walking eight miles each day selling eggs house to house from his family farm and investing his profit in a candy business. He was only fifteen when he invented his ear protector, and if the children initially snickered at his contraption, it wasn't for long. Soon everyone wanted a pair.

Encouraged by his friends' interest, Chester worked to improve and refine his design, changing the farm wire to spring steel, which could be coiled flat, and adding a small hinge that kept the muff snug against each ear.

On March 13, 1877, the United States Patent Office awarded eighteen-year-old Chester Greenwood patent no. 188,292 for his invention; for the next sixty years the manufacture of Greenwood's Champion Ear Protectors was Chester's chief occupation. In 1881 he built a factory in West Farmington and later expanded into Farmington Village. By 1883, 30,000 pairs of earmuffs were being produced. Production increased rapidly during World War I, when the factory began supplying U.S. soldiers with earmuffs, and by 1936, with the introduction of new, bright fabrics, more than 400,000 pairs were being shipped. The factory employed dozens of local women in Franklin County; they took the piecework home to hand-sew fabric to the hinged flap, just as Chester's grandmother had done years earlier.

By the time of his death in 1937, Chester had become a local celebrity, a man who not only epitomized the hardy, industrious New England spirit, but also embodied the ideals of good citizenry. A father of four and a lover of the outdoors, he was generous, patient, and humble by nature. Devoted to his community, he was active in the Farmington Grange, Franklin Lodge no. 58, his Unitarian church, and the local school board. His quiet, inventive genius was recognized during his lifetime with more than one hundred patents.

In 1977 the Maine State Legislature paid tribute to Chester Greenwood by declaring December 21 Chester Greenwood Day throughout the State of Maine.

> December 21st of each year shall be designated as Chester Greenwood Day and the Governor shall annually issue a proclamation inviting and urging the people of the State of Maine to observe this day in suitable places with appropriate ceremony and activity. Chester Greenwood Day shall commemorate and honor Chester Greenwood, whose inventive genius and native ability, which contributed much to the enjoyment of Maine's winter season, marked him as one of Maine's outstanding citizens.

The citizens of tiny Farmington—population 7,500—still pay tribute to their favorite son with an annual Chester Greenwood Day parade on the first Saturday in December, a cherished rite of the Christmas season for which everyone and everything—police cars, fire trucks, cows, and plows—come dressed in earmuffs. The Chester Greenwood flag is raised at the Superior Court building, and Chester Greenwood memorabilia is on display. Members of the extended Greenwood family come home for the holiday to enjoy chili, hot chocolate, and birthday cake with townspeople at the gazebo and to remember the man whose full and useful life made Farmington the "Earmuff Capital of the World."

The Christmas Blizzard of 1909

WITH A TRACE of snow on the ground and another half-inch dusting on Christmas morning, it was just barely a white Christmas that December 25, 1909. Little did anyone realize that a behemoth was bearing down on New England. It began later on Christmas night, a Saturday, and didn't end until twenty-four hours later. When it finally departed in the wee hours of Monday morning, December 27, the great brooding storm had left a trail of ruin. The wind, the tide, and the snow had wreaked havoc enough to paralyze New England and earn the blizzard, a classic nor'easter, a place in New England weather history.

The normal eleven-foot tide in Boston Harbor was sixteen feet. Not since 1851 had the tide been that high. All along the coast, waves inundated warehouses and bridges, washed out piers, destroyed breakwaters, and carried

Snow shovels. Courtesy Boston Public Library Print Department.

away beach cottages. Boats were smashed on beaches. Gas lines were flooded as streets were covered by a foot of water.

Heavy snow crippled services. Fire alarms, telephones, streetlights, and telegraphs were all down. As trolley lines fell into the snow, the sparking wires, noted one newspaper reporter, looked like a pyrotechnics show.

Early Monday morning, as the snow clouds passed, a full moon shone forth in a cloudless sky. Moonbeams turned the countryside silver, and with the sunrise came an autumnal gold. As day broke, the world was brilliantly, dazzlingly white and calm.

Touched by an Angel: Larkin Mead Jr.

ONE HUNDRED FIFTY years ago, the village of Brattleboro, Vermont, was touched by an angel. It was in December 1856, on the dark eve of the New Year, that the angelic figure appeared at the junction of North Main and Linden Streets. Eight feet tall, she was sculpted of snow and glazed with ice that gave her a sparkling luster.

As the new day and the New Year dawned bright and clear, the people of Brattleboro discovered the angel

> in the prismatic glow of the morning sun's reflection. The early risers and pedestrians about town were amazed, when they drew near, to see what appeared at a distance like a schoolboy's work turned to a statue of such exquisite contour and grace of form, with such delicate mouldings and dimplings in detail as to suggest the use of a chisel, and that only in a master hand. There was a serious face, rounded arms, neck and bust and waving drapery. It was a noble conception; the young sculptor had evidently endeavored to embody the serious thought which visits us while we look backward and forward from the line which separates a dawning and a dying year. The passing schoolboy was awed for once, as he viewed the result of adept handling of the elements with which he was so roughly familiar, and the thought of snowballing so beautiful an object could never have dwelt in his mind.

The young creator of this "Recording Angel," she who kept a general account of the deeds of the past year by marking them on her tablet, was Larkin Goldsmith Mead Jr., a Brattleboro lad whose Snow Angel would bring him national attention and launch his career as a sculptor.

Born in Chesterfield, New Hampshire, in 1835, Mead moved to Brattleboro with his family when he was four. Early on he displayed a talent for drawing and sculpting and caught the eye of an art teacher who was in Brat-

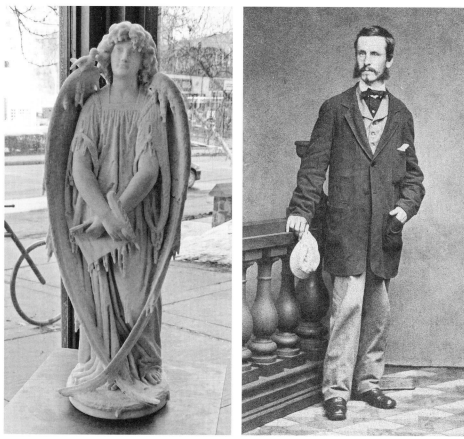

Snow Angel, by Larkin G. Mead Jr. Courtesy Brooks Memorial Library, Brattleboro, Vermont.

Larkin G. Mead Jr. as he appeared on his *carte de visite,* 1862. Courtesy Miscellaneous Photograph Collection, Archives of American Art/Smithsonian Institution.

tleboro taking the water cure. At nineteen, Mead began art studies in New York, returning in 1856 to Brattleboro, where he opened his own drawing school.

On the evening of what many later said was his divine inspiration, Mead and two companions labored for hours by lantern light in the bitter cold, in a snowdrift, kneading and molding the snow. A fire burning in the nearby foundry melted the snow that glazed the statue. Cold weather—and what accounts of the day said was "respect generally accorded to genius"—allowed the Snow Angel to survive, in all her perfect splendor, for nearly two weeks. The writer James Russell Lowell later noted, "It was a pretty fancy of the young Vermont sculptor to make his first essay in this evanescent material."

Snowrolling, 1940. Courtesy Vermont State Archives.

But it was not Mead's last essay. Many prestigious commissions followed, including one for a marble replica of the Snow Angel, another for a full-length statue of Ethan Allen and a statue of Abraham Lincoln. After working on the front during the Civil War as an artist for *Harper's Weekly,* Mead moved to Italy, first to Venice and later to Florence, where he made his permanent home and worked as a respected artist for more than fifty years. He made frequent visits to Brattleboro before his death in 1910.

Dashing thro' the Snow

IF, THESE DAYS, the very mention of a snowstorm sends some New Englanders into a tizzy, if a few inches of the white stuff brings everything to a standstill, or at least a crawl, it wasn't always that way. Back in the days of horses and sleighs, a thick blanket of fresh snow was a welcome event; it resculpted the landscape, turning rocky, potholed, muddy roads and impassable meadows, woods, and ponds into a network of sleighing thoroughfares.

Today the sleigh ride has become something of a novelty, a winter amusement offered to guests—along with a thick woolen blanket and a mug of steaming hot chocolate—at inns and Christmas tree farms. But in times past, the sleigh—or sledge—one of the world's oldest means of transportation, was the only way to get from place to place when the snow piled up.

Christmas Belles, by Winslow Homer. From *Harper's Weekly,* 1869. Courtesy Dover Publications.

Left on roadways and packed down with horse-drawn rollers, snow was anything but an impediment to travel; it made travel easier. Snow was freedom, saving folks from a winter of cabin fever.

With the harvest in and work done for the season, wintertime—especially the holiday season—was a time for socializing, for visiting friends and family—often separated by great distances—as well as traveling to local inns and taverns, then the heart of a town's political and social life. For farmers who needed to transport heavy materials such as lumber, and for merchants who had goods to deliver, the sleigh was a practical and utilitarian vehicle, but for young people, it was the equivalent of a modern sports car. Often homemade and elaborately decorated, the sleigh was an indispensable social and recreational vehicle, used for courting, for moonlit and lantern-lit rides to barn dances, for sleighing parties, and for cutter races, the last a popular winter pastime that drew crowds of spectators along the main thoroughfares between rival towns.

With the advent of automobiles and a much improved roadway system, sleighs were no longer a necessity, though in some rural areas of New England they continued to be used long after town and city folk had dismissed them as relics of a bygone time. There's still an allure about sleighing that suggests warmth, togetherness, and conviviality. James Pierpont's "Jingle Bells," as well as Leroy Anderson's "Sleigh Ride," fondly evoke the olden days, days of runners "hissing" on the snow, of whinnying horses, of muffs and blankets, and strands of sleigh bells—without which Christmas just wouldn't be Christmas.

Sleighing on Beacon Street, 1910. Courtesy Boston Public Library Print Department.

Jordan Marsh Nativity scene, c. 1950. Courtesy Boston Public Library Print Department.

VIII. How We Celebrate the Season

SINCE THE ANCIENT, dark days, the midwinter season has been a time to celebrate. Whether with great, public festivals or quiet gatherings at home, Christmas has been, and continues to be, a time for fellowship and sharing.

The ways that New Englanders celebrate the season are as diverse as New Englanders themselves, and if few feel the need to coax the sun back to strength or placate the gods, most still feel the need for traditions, for the rituals that bind them to the past and to one another.

Like our forebears, we honor Christmas Eve as the most hallowed, mysterious day of the season, the day when the Gospel tells of angels appearing to the shepherds to herald the birth of Christ. Folklore, too, spoke of Christmas Eve as being a magical night, a night when animals spoke and knelt in their stalls toward the east. Well water was said to turn to wine. In long-lost valleys, church bells could be heard pealing on Christmas Eve.

In the more modern era, Christmas Eve is still a night to share with wildlife and pets. It is still a night to leave tables set and front doors unlocked to welcome departed family members or the visitor in need of food and shelter. It is the night, in so many places, to trim the tree, to hang the stockings, to eat the grand meal, the night when carolers and bell ringers stroll from house to house and when children eagerly await their favorite gift giver.

Christmas Eve was the night, too, when, in an extraordinary display of shared humanity, French and German soldiers came under the day's spell and declared a truce in 1914, setting aside differences for one evening and the following day until, sadly, the terrible fighting resumed.

One thing is certain: since time immemorial, the antidote to the physical and spiritual cold and dark of the midwinter season has been fellowship and forgiveness, generosity and goodwill. If over the years in some ways much has changed, in other ways very little has.

The Shakers: A Gift to Be Simple

AT A TIME when most of New England considered December 25 to be just another workday (unless it fell on the Sabbath), throughout New England small, peaceful Utopian communities of semimonastic Christians called Shakers were "keeping the day."

The Shakers, named by "outsiders" for their jubilant expressions of faith, were more formally known as the United Society of Believers in Christ's Second Appearing. Separatists who had first organized in Manchester, England, in 1747, they were persecuted for their beliefs, but they found a charismatic leader in Ann Lee (1736–84), a working-class woman whom they believed to be imbued by Christ's spirit. In 1774 a revelation from heaven brought Mother Ann and eight followers to America, an America that was undergoing its own emancipation. They settled in an area near the Hudson River, empty but for swamp and forest, called Niskeyuna.

In this country Mother Ann sought to establish a community, a "Heaven on Earth," without violence, corruption, poverty, and the evils that had plagued the Old World they had fled. Despite being harassed, imprisoned, and driven from town to town in America, over time the Shakers were able to attract converts and establish eighteen self-contained agricultural communities in Maine, New Hampshire, Massachusetts, Connecticut, New York, Kentucky, Ohio, Indiana, Georgia, and Florida. At their height just before the Civil War, the Shakers numbered between four thousand and six thousand adherents who shared the basic principles of pacifism, celibacy, gender equality, public confession of sin, repentance, communitarian life, and, above all else, the oneness of God.

From their first winter in Niskeyuna (later named Watervliet), the Shakers made Christmas the highlight of their year. Mother Ann believed she had been given a spiritual sign when Sister Hannah Hocknell, shaking from the cold, had been unable to put on her shoes for a day of housework. It was December 25, 1776, and Ann saw it as a calling to set aside one day of the year for the inner "work" of spiritual housecleaning, repentance, and rebirth.

The earliest Christmases were spent quietly, fasting, nurturing love and respect for one another, and giving relationships that might have suffered

Shaker Sister Mamie Curtis with a Christmas tree, 1910. Collection of the United
Society of Shakers, Sabbathday Lake, Maine.

during the year a second chance. There were no special meals or festivities, though small handmade gifts—tokens of love, given in love—were exchanged. Over time, however, the Shaker Christmas began to reflect many of the festivities and traditions that "outsiders" associated with the day.

At the Sabbathday Lake village in New Gloucester, Maine, preparations for Christmas began weeks ahead of time, and the air, it was said, became "quite heavy with Merry Christmases." Goose and turkey were dressed, pies, cookies, and cakes baked, cornballs made, and the best apples, sweetest jellies, and spiciest pickles were set aside for the Christmas Eve smorgasbord. Simple, haunting songs that touched the heart were written and prepared in secret—to be sung only on Christmas Day—by special groups within the community. The entertainment also included a pageant, written by the Shakers or ordered from commercial publishers. Costumes were sewn, backdrops constructed, and rehearsals held, all in secret so as to surprise the family, as they call their community.

Fresh greens were gathered. A tree, cut from the woods by the Shaker boys, was decorated with wax candles and ornaments and installed in the

Sister Frances's Fruitcake

1 cup raisins	½ teaspoon nutmeg
1 cup water	1 egg, beaten
½ cup shortening	1 teaspoon baking soda
1 cup sugar	½ teaspoon salt
1 teaspoon cinnamon	2 scant cups flour
½ teaspoon cloves	Fruit and nuts for topping

In a large saucepan combine the raisins, water, shortening, sugar, and spices. Boil for 20 minutes and cool. Then add the remaining ingredients. Pour into a greased tube pan and decorate with dried fruits and pecan halves. Bake at 350° or 375° for 45 minutes.

communal dining room, the center of daily life. Tables were filled with "needful" and "useful" presents and walls were adorned with beautiful mottoes to remind everyone of the occasion. A fast day—the true Christmas gift—was observed on a Sunday before Christmas, a day "sacredly kept and devoted to personal examination."

Small bags of candy—brittle, caramels, and chocolates—were prepared for friends and relatives. Stockings were hung on the children's bedposts waiting to be filled by Santa Claus, the universal symbol of love. The entry from the *Sabbathday Lake Church Record and Journal* for December 25, 1895, reflects the Shaker embrace of a typical New England Christmas: "The children, both boys and girls hung their stockings and found them quite well filled this morning. Santa Claus does not forget."

The last active community of Shakers, that at Sabbathday Lake, continues to devote its work to God and to prepare every December for the intangible gifts of the season. Always deeply concerned about the plight of children, many of whom, orphaned and abandoned, found a loving home with the Shakers until the early 1960s, the Shakers of Sabbathday Lake—in the spirit of Christmas, when a child was born—continue their outreach on behalf of children.

The Annual Shaker Christmas Fair at Sabbathday Lake, held on the first Saturday in December, is an eagerly awaited event attended by friends and neighbors who happily carry home tins of herbs, pickles, baked goods, fancy goods, candies, fresh cider, and cheese. Warm biscuits are served from the Shaker kitchen throughout the day, and Sister Frances's fruitcake is, by all accounts, a hands-down winner.

The Shaker culture is one in which work is worship, in which the material gifts the Shakers have given the world express the beauty, simplicity, practicality, grace, and purity of their spirituality. Their belief that we can all receive a spark of the divine if we are receptive is never truer than at Christmas.

Captain James Magee's Holiday Party

ON THE NIGHT of Friday, December 25, 1778, Captain James Magee, a "convivial, noble-hearted Irishman" originally from County Down, was commanding the hundred-foot brigantine *General Arnold* when he made a fateful decision. With a violent snowstorm bearing down, the twenty-eight-year-old Magee sought refuge for his vessel and its crew of 105 at anchor in Plymouth Harbor. Another privateer, the *Revenge*, was caught in the same storm, but made a different decision—to ride out the storm off Cape Cod. The *Revenge* survived the storm intact; the *General Arnold* met a disastrous fate.

That night gale winds ripped the *General Arnold* loose from its anchors and drove the vessel onto White Flat. For thirty-six hours waves relentlessly pounded the *General Arnold,* breaking it in two and burying it deeper in the sand. Though the ship was only a mile from shore and within plain view, the dreadful weather and intense cold prevented any rescue attempts. Desperate, the seamen broke into casks of brandy; though Captain Magee pleaded with them to pour the brandy into their boots to prevent frostbite, the men instead consumed the "liquid warmth," which rendered them even more vulnerable to the cold. Together they huddled in subfreezing temperatures; not until Monday, the fourth day, were rescuers able to reach them. By then seventy of the men had frozen to death; another thirteen died soon after their rescue.

In 1832, in his *History of the Town of Plymouth,* James Thacher recounted the tragedy, noting that the vessel "soon filled with water and it became necessary to cut away the masts. . . . A tremendous storm of wind and snow came on, and a considerable number of men died on Saturday afternoon and in the night. . . . Sunday morning, the vessel was seen in a most distressful situation, enveloped in ice and snow, and the whole shore was frozen to a solid body of ice, the winds and waves raging with such dreadful violence that no possible relief could be afforded to the miserable sufferers."

Of the surviving seamen, all except Magee were crippled for life by severe frostbite. Magee, though physically unscathed, would be haunted for the rest of his life by the loss of his crew and his fateful decision of December 25, 1778.

For several years after the wreck of the *General Arnold*, Captain Magee continued to serve the Patriot cause and later commanded merchant ships out of Salem, Massachusetts. In 1783 he married Margaret Elliot, with whom he had nine children; six years later Captain Magee was at the helm of the vessel *Astrea* when it sailed into Canton, China, one of the first ships to begin American trade with China. During the 1790s Magee became a prominent figure in the China trade and a wealthy man.

Despite his comfortable life, Captain Magee never forgot the stormy night of December 25, 1778, or the crew of the ill-fated *General Arnold*. While living on Boston's Federal Street and, later, at the elegant Shirley Place in Boston's fashionable Roxbury neighborhood, Captain Magee hosted holiday parties for the surviving crew members and their families and for the widows and children of those lost. Accepting full responsibility for the fate of the *General Arnold*, Captain Magee endeavored to assist the families in any way he could. When he died in 1801 at the age of fifty-one—some said because of his lifetime of anguish—Captain Magee was buried, as he had requested, with his crew on Burial Hill in Plymouth, where an obelisk marks the graves of those who died on the *General Arnold*.

Today, every December, as a way of remembering and honoring the "convivial, noble-hearted Irishman" and celebrating the Christmas season as Captain Magee and his family would have two hundred years ago, the trustees of Shirley Place—now the Shirley-Eustis House—host the annual Captain Magee's Holiday Party, an afternoon of contradancing and fiddle music, fruitcakes, meringues, macaroons, ginger cookies, and mincemeat tarts, and a potent brandy and rum punch—Fish House punch—that Captain Magee would have loved.

The imposing Shirley-Eustis House, built by Royal Governor William Shirley between 1747 and 1751 and now the sole remaining country estate built in America by a royal colonial governor, is today a National Historic Landmark. The house is tucked into the busy, urban, diverse Dudley Street

Captain Magee's Eighteenth-Century Fish House Punch

Mix together the juice of 12 lemons (1½ cups) and several spoonfuls powdered sugar

> Add 1½ quarts brandy
>
> 1 pint peach brandy
>
> 1 pint rum
>
> 1 quart carbonated water
>
> 1 quart brewed tea

Add more tea, lemon juice, or water to taste.

Stir well and add slices of oranges.

Serves 18

neighborhood in Roxbury; its extensive orchards, bucolic landscape, and fine harbor view may be gone, but at Christmastime, when the house is decorated simply but elegantly with greens and wreaths and centerpieces of lemons and pineapples, the spirit of Captain Magee—and the men of the *General Arnold*—lives on.

Meninho Jesu: *The Little Jesus*

IN THE TINY Portuguese fishing village of Provincetown on Cape Cod, only today's oldest citizens remember when the workmen of the Provincetown Light and Power Company decorated their home office for Christmas and strung Commercial Street in curving garlands of colored lights. In front of Town Hall, a little tree laden with lights—Provincetown's "official tree"—blazed brightly, and every window on every house, it seemed, glowed with warm candlelight. On High Pole Hill, the Pilgrim Monument was illuminated from top to bottom with floodlights and strung on four sides with colored lights. From out at sea the little town must have looked like a shining beacon, a symbol of the hope and ideals of the season.

A feeling of neighborliness and goodwill filled the air in the weeks before Christmas. Families were busy gathering berries and evergreen boughs in

Meninho Jesu. Courtesy Father Manuel Pereira.

the woods, baking elaborate treats, and knitting and sewing gifts. There was always a little something for everyone, even if it was only a small token of friendship.

In every Portuguese home, in a front room, families kept an altar, a pyramid of lace-covered graduated shelves on which delicate figures of Mary, Joseph, the baby Jesus, the Magi, shepherds, and angels were displayed. Predating the Christmas tree, pyramids were common in European culture—the Italians called theirs a *ceppo,* the Germans a *lichtstock*—and with their burning candles were the forerunners to the lighted Christmas tree.

The Portuguese called their altar *Meninho Jesu,* Little Jesus, and lovingly ornamented it with cherished family heirlooms, small religious statues and Nativity figurines that had been carried from the Old World and passed down through the generations, and with flowers, evergreens, a crucifix, and candles to represent the Resurrection and the Light. Small pots of freshly sprouted wheat, planted weeks earlier and kept in the dark to grow white, were set out to symbolize the living body of Christ. The *Meninho Jesu* was the centerpiece of every Portuguese home.

On Christmas Eve, after the family had lighted the candles on the *Meninho Jesu,* gaily decorated homes were thrown open to friends and strangers alike. No invitation was ever needed and indeed, as Mary Heaton Vorse wrote in her Provincetown chronicle, *Time and the Town,* "the most welcome and honored guests were the strangers."

Musicians strolled the streets, playing Old World accordions and guitars and singing Old World songs. One song asked for permission to enter the home to visit the *Meninho Jesu.* Another was a tender cradle song, sung to the infant Jesus.

Visiting from house to house, friends and strangers would invariably ask if the baby was wet, "Ou meninho miza?"—which was a roundabout way of asking, "Is there liquor available?"—and guests would be treated to a glass of homemade wine brewed from beach plums, blueberries, or cracked corn in backyard stills. The large dining room table would be spread with dozens of gorgeous cookies, with sweet potato turnovers called trutas, soufflés, meringues, and lemon tarts, with cranberry sauce, bowls of fava beans, marinated shrimp, pickled onions, steamed chestnuts, steamers, quahogs, linguica, and sweet breads.

At midnight, after a night of making merry, folks made their way, in a bond of fellowship, to the mass at the Episcopal Church of St. Mary's of the Harbor. Before the Catholic Church introduced its midnight service, Portuguese and Yankee, Catholic and Protestant alike, filled the pews at St. Mary's. In the spirit of the season, they set aside whatever differences there may have been to celebrate, as one community, the birthday of the Lord.

One Enchanted Evening

ENCHANTED VILLAGE began, as so many magical things do, as one man's dream of what Christmas could and should be. For many years the Jordan Marsh Company—the "Mercantile Heart of New England"—in downtown Boston epitomized the Christmas spirit of giving and sharing. It was the first store in America to clear its expansive street-level windows of store merchandise and celebrate the Christmas season with a life-sized Nativity scene. For years Jordan's fleet of trucks—its Christmas caravan— bedecked with decorations and loaded with Santa and gifts, traveled the city, visiting children in hospitals and orphanages.

In 1958 Jordan's president, Edward Mitton, had an idea for an even more ambitious gift for the boys and girls of New England. He envisioned a

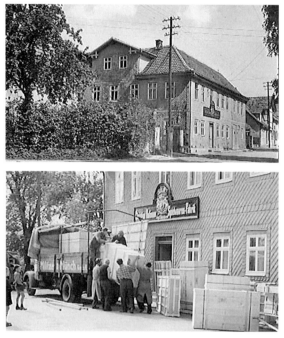

Promotional piece for the Jordan Marsh Enchanted Village, 1959.
Courtesy Christian Hofmann Company, Germany.

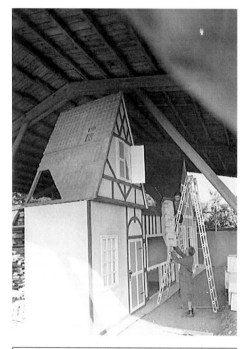

(ABOVE) The construction of Jordan Marsh
Enchanted Village at Christian Hofmann
Company, 1959. Courtesy Christian Hofmann
Company, Germany.

(LEFT) Enchanted Village ticket.
Private collection.

Santa's village, built to a child's scale—4'8"—installed during the Christmas season in his downtown store. To realize his dream, he turned to the toy makers and master craftsmen of the Christian Hofmann Company in the tiny German village of Rodach, near Coburg in Bavaria, to design and build the Enchanted Village of St. Nicholas.

For nearly a century, the artisans at Christian Hofmann had been acknowledged as the masters in animated display figures. Still, for Hofmann and for Jordan Marsh, the Enchanted Village of St. Nicholas would be the most ambitious project ever undertaken.

In March 1959 work began on the village. The Christian Hofmann Company added 8,500 square feet of floor space to its factory, as well as dozens of skilled carpenters, doll makers, and painters to its staff. More than 45,000 man-hours were spent creating twenty-eight heartwarming scenes, 250 figures, and 16,200 mechanical parts. More than 4,000 feet of wire were used, 160 motors, and 100 gallons of paint. When the village was ready for delivery to Boston, all 80,000 pounds of Santa's friends, helpers, and their pets were packed into 240 cartons and shipped across the Atlantic.

Meanwhile, in Boston Jordan Marsh employees were preparing a new 10,000-square-foot space for the village. Eighteen feet high and three hundred feet long, the Enchanted Village of St. Nicholas, with its general store, bakery, shoemaker's shop, glassblower's shop, and schoolhouse, its poinsettias, holly balls, tarts, pies, and a sled named Rosebud, opened its doors to the children of New England for the Christmas season. Every one of the twenty-eight scenes featured some animation. From a tiny mouse to a toy soldier's moustache, there were eighty-six moving parts in all.

In his dedication of the Enchanted Village of St. Nicholas, Edward Mitton noted that "this delightful, authentic panorama, with its wonderful animated characters at work and play, is for the enjoyment of all children and adults. We hope it will cast its spell of enchantment over all our New England friends . . . adding to a brighter, gayer, more delightful Christmas season . . . for everyone!"

For New England children coming of age in the 1960s, visiting the Enchanted Village of St. Nicholas—beginning with a stop to pick up a free ticket from one of Santa's elves at the ticket booth on the corner of Chauncey and Summer Streets—became a cherished Christmas tradition. The magical visit was often capped off with a visit to Bailey's Ice Cream Shop for a hot fudge sundae.

By the early 1970s economic recession had put a crimp in retailing, and Jordan Marsh reluctantly discontinued its Christmas display. Packed away, the Enchanted Village seemed all but forgotten until 1990, when Macy's took over Jordan Marsh and began to display the village. The children of the 1960s, with a sparkle in their eyes, were now moms and dads bringing a whole new generation to see the Enchanted Village, hoping that it would again work its magic on young and old alike.

In 1998 Macy's donated the Enchanted Village to the City of Boston, and Mayor Thomas Menino kept a tradition alive by installing the display in a heated, domed structure on City Hall Plaza. In 2003, with the expense of maintaining the village mounting, the mayor reluctantly announced that the city would no longer be able to afford the installation and staffing of the display. The citizens of New England—many who remembered every detail about the village and who equated its loss with the loss of Christmas itself—would hear nothing of its demise and stepped up with donations.

Now in its new home at the John B. Hynes Veterans Memorial Convention Center, on Boylston Street in the Back Bay, the Enchanted Village of St. Nicholas continues to delight New Englanders of all ages, offering a vision of a simpler time, not only a time when a wreath could be bought for five cents or when streets were illuminated with gas lamps, but a time when a cheery mechanical boy waving an ice cream scoop and a little girl buying a yard of special cherry red ribbon (an homage to Jordan Marsh's founder, Eben Jordan, whose very first sale back in the early 1850s was a yard of cherry red ribbon) were enough to captivate children and make them believe that the Enchanted Village was their own magical world.

Bailey's Hot Fudge Sauce

2 squares (2 ounces) unsweetened baking chocolate
½ cup butter
2 cups confectioner's sugar
¾ cup evaporated milk

Melt butter and chocolate over low heat. Remove from heat. Add sugar and milk alternately and stir until smooth. Simmer for 8–10 minutes.

The Christmas Parish: Holy Trinity German Church

THE CHRISTMAS PARISH, Holy Trinity Church—Heilige Dreifaltigkeits Kirche—was never a church like others in the Boston Archdiocese. In its heyday its pews were crowded with families named Kramer, Muller, Plumer, Schmitt, Wessling, Herr, Burkhart, and Dorr, families that had left their German homeland to start a new life in a New World, families that kept Christmas long before most in New England did. The first ethnic Catholic group in the Boston Archdiocese, German immigrants began arriving as early as the late 1820s. Many continued their journey westward, but thousands remained in Boston, a Brahmin and soon-to-be Irish enclave, where they faced a language barrier and a new social environment, still influenced largely by Puritanism, that threatened German traditions, including the cherished celebration of Christmas, toward which antipathy was still deeply ingrained in New England.

For all newly arrived immigrants to America, local parishes became safe havens not only for spiritual needs, but for social needs as well. Though Boston's Irish Catholic pastors did what they could for German Catholic immigrants, they were unable to hear confessions and give counsel. German immigrants well understood the importance of learning English and assimilating into Boston society, but they feared that without a church of their own they would quickly lose their language and their Old World customs.

In 1844 Holy Trinity Church, a National German Catholic Church with German clergy, was founded in Boston's South End. Where most Roman Catholic churches served the neighborhood around the parish, Holy Trinity Church was unique in serving anyone of German ancestry. That same year Holy Trinity parishioners opened New England's first parochial school, for both boys and girls. There followed other schools, a home for elderly widows, and an

Old Holy Trinity German Church, 1860.
Courtesy Boston Public Library Print Department.

orphanage. In a short time Holy Trinity became much more than a church. It became a way of life, a place not only for spiritual nurturing, but for social support and educational opportunity as well.

By the 1870s, in the aftermath of war in Europe, more than seven thousand Germans were living in Boston, a number that grew to more than ten thousand by the turn of the century. To accommodate the growing German immigrant community, a grand, new Gothic church was planned; in November 1872, just days after the Great Boston Fire, its cornerstone was laid.

The first mass in the new church was celebrated in the basement on May 1, 1874, and on May 27, 1877, the feast of the Holy Trinity, the new Holy Trinity Church, designed by the preeminent neo-Gothic church architect, Patrick Keely, was dedicated on Shawmut Avenue. The church, like its predecessor, was constructed of Roxbury puddingstone and Maine granite. With its German stained-glass windows and carved wooden statuary, it had an Old World ambience and warmth. Its slender steeple graced the skyline of Boston's South End until it was damaged during the 1938 hurricane—and never replaced.

For the German faithful at Holy Trinity, few occasions during the year were more joyous than Christmas, always celebrated with a high mass at midnight, a candlelit shepherds' procession, and carols on Christmas Eve. In 1966 Holy Trinity's organist and music director, George Krim, revived the nineteenth-century tradition of a Christmas pageant, said to have had its American beginnings at Holy Trinity Church. His lavish, spiritual masterwork, *A Christmas Tableau in Five Settings,* designed for a cast of silent, costumed actors and a choir of seventy voices, helped to restore Holy Trinity's reputation as the "Christmas Parish." Performed at Epiphany on alternate years, the pageant told the Christmas story, from Christ's birth to the Epiphany, with music and readings from the Scripture.

If the tableau was spiritually uplifting in all its elaborate pageantry, midnight mass on Christmas Eve was uplifting in all its elegant simplicity. The church was dark but for candles in the windows and on the altar, where, a Christmas tree also twinkled in lights. Parishioners joined in singing German carols, and in the echoes of "Stille Nacht," first sung in Austria on Christmas Eve in 1818, there could be heard the ancestral voices of those first émigrés who had braved the New World.

Though Holy Trinity's pastoral mission has changed since the early days of German immigration, its proud legacy of service and support to the community has not. It has become home to the Latin mass community and to the Cardinal Medeiros Center and Bridge over Troubled Waters, two social services agencies serving the homeless of Boston. The German—and Holy Trinity's—contribution to New England's rich diversity and to its Christmas traditions will be remembered whenever Christmas trees are decorated with glass ornaments, when cards are sent and received, and when voices are raised in the singing of "Silent Night" in the silent night.

> *Stille Nacht! heilige Nacht!*
> *Alles schläft; einsam wacht*
> *Nur das traute heilige Paar.*
> > *Holder Knab im lockigten Harr,*
> > *Schlafe in himmlischer Ruh!*
> > *Schlafe in himmlischer Ruh!*

(Holy Trinity German Church is one of the parishes the Boston Archdiocese intends to close as part of its cost-cutting plan. Originally scheduled to close on June 30, 2005, the church remains open and continues to serve the community.)

Stir Up, We Beseech Thee: Trinity Church, Newport

FEW TRADITIONS EVOKE an old fashioned Dickensian Christmas more than the sight of a blazing plum pudding, with its signature sprig of holly for protection and good luck, presented as the grand finale of a sumptuous Christmas dinner. Though costly and time-consuming to make, the plum pudding was a necessary finish to every old English Christmas, a once-a-year treat, wrapped and boiled in a dishcloth, which even a struggling family like Bob Cratchit's could not bear to do without.

> Hallo! A great deal of steam! The pudding was out of the copper. A smell like a washing-day! That was the cloth. A smell like an eating-house and a pastry-cook's next door to each other with a laundress's next door to that! That was the pudding! In half a minute Mrs. Cratchit entered—flushed but smiling proudly—with the pudding, like a speckled cannon-ball, so hard and firm, blazing in half of half a quartern of ignited brandy, and bedight with Christmas holly stuck into the top.
>
> Oh, a wonderful pudding! Bob Cratchit said, and calmly, too, that he regarded it as the greatest success achieved by Mrs. Cratchit since their marriage.

Plum pudding—which does not use plums but derives its name from the plumping of the raisins—evolved from the ancient pagan dish frumenty, or furmety, a spiced porridge made from the sacred wheat and stirred up by the harvest god, Dagda, who added chopped fruits and meats to symbolize all the goodness of the Earth. By the late seventeenth century the dish had been sweetened and thickened into the rich, dark—and filling—traditional pudding of English country life. Silver charms—a coin symbolizing wealth; a button, bachelorhood; a thimble, spinsterhood; and a ring, marriage—were baked into the pudding and presaged the future for whoever might bite into one.

In a certain sense, it took a village to make a Christmas pudding. On the first Sunday in Advent (the fourth Sunday before Christmas), neighbors joined together at the local parish to make the Christmas pudding, each contributing one of the many ingredients: the butcher the suet, the farmer the eggs, the grocer the fruits. While reciting the collect from the Book of Common Prayer for that day—"Stir up, we beseech thee, O Lord, the hearts of thy faithful people; that they, plenteously bringing forth the fruits of good works, may by thee be plenteously rewarded; Amen"—a reminder that it was time to make the puddings, each member of the parish family took a ritual turn with the spoon, stirring the thick batter—always in a clockwise direction so as not to invite evil spirits—until the eggs and fruit, suet and bread crumbs, were all well blended.

That old spirit of community survives at the historic Trinity Church in Newport, Rhode Island, where, sometime in mid-December, on Plum Pudding Stir Sunday, members of the church family take their turn with the spoon. Though some commercial bakers offer a "figgy" pudding at Christmastime, there is, say parishioners, nothing quite like one made the old-fashioned way, from a recipe said to have come to Newport from England in 1730 and handed down through the generations.

There's no rushing a plum pudding. The batter, to properly ripen, should be made weeks ahead of Christmas, which gives the brandy time to soak into the fruits. Steaming a plum pudding takes hours—and patience— so that the suet slowly and thoroughly dissolves. The suet is no ordinary suet that one might put out for the birds, but the special fat that surrounds a cow's kidneys, generally available only from specialty butchers.

Because they use their plum puddings for fund-raising for the church choir, Trinity Church parishioners actually prepare their batter in November, ahead of Stir Sunday. Most of the batter is separated into small, individual containers, but a large ceremonial bowl of batter is saved for Plum

Hurrah for the Pudding! From *Little Folks*, c. 1870. Courtesy Dover Publications.

Trinity Church Plum Pudding

1 pound dry bread crumbs rolled fine (about 4 cups)

4 cups flour	2 pounds seedless raisins
1 pound sugar (2 cups)	½ pound mixed chopped candied peel
1 teaspoon salt	2 cups chopped peeled apples
1 tablespoon cinnamon	12 eggs
1 tablespoon grated nutmeg	Grated rind and juice of 2 lemons
2 pounds finely chopped or ground suet	½ cup brandy
2 pounds currants	1 cup good sweet cider

Mix dry ingredients well, adding suet and fruits. Beat eggs thoroughly and to them add liquids, including lemon juice and rind. Add to dry ingredients and mix well.

Pour mixture into small, well-greased bowls or pudding molds (the recipe will make three large puddings or five or six medium-size puddings). Bowls should be no more than two-thirds full. Cover the bowls with greased muslin cloth or heavy waxed paper. Tie covers on with string.

Wishing you Plenty of Christmas Cheer, and a Happy, Contented Time through the New Year

Christmas greeting, c. 1960.
Private collection.

Put bowls in steamer or on rack in pan of boiling water, which should come about three-fourths of the way up the bowl or mold.

Cover pan, return water to boil, then reduce heat to lowest point and steam for three hours, keeping water at simmer. Remove puddings and let them cool to room temperature. Keep puddings tightly covered and refrigerate. Will keep for up to a year.

To reheat, steam the covered pudding in its mold or bowl as described above for about an hour. Turn finished pudding onto a plate. Heat ¼ cup brandy, pour over pudding, and light. (If you have decorated the plate with holly, be careful with flames, for the holly may burn.)

Serve the pudding with plenty of good brandy sauce.

Brandy Sauce

1 cup sugar	2 eggs, beaten
⅓ cup butter, softened	1 teaspoon vanilla
1 cup heavy cream	4 tablespoons brandy

Cream sugar and butter. Add eggs and cream. Cook over low heat until slightly thickened. Do not boil.

Add vanilla and brandy.

Make the sauce ahead of time and warm over hot water just before serving.

Pudding Stir Sunday. On that day, following the custom in early English churches, Trinity parishioners stir the batter, each making a wish during his or her turn, on their way out of church. With ceremony befitting the event, they are greeted by committee members in colonial dress and by members of the Newport Artillery, the oldest military organization in the United States. The church choir entertains with carols. Refreshments are served, including a taste of steaming pudding drizzled with brandy sauce. For sale are the individual puddings that were set aside weeks earlier.

It seems fitting that plum pudding, outlawed in Puritan England for its pagan origins, should today be so much a part of Newport's Christmas celebration. It was Puritan excess and intolerance in Massachusetts that drove many colonists to Rhode Island in search of religious tolerance, and in every spoonful of plum pudding there is tradition as well as a taste of defiance.

Turtle Frolic

IN DAYS PAST, for the well-to-do in seaport towns such as Newport, Rhode Island, few things were more eagerly awaited, more welcome, than the delivery of a giant sea turtle from the West Indies.

Since ancient times, the flesh and eggs of the sea turtle had been esteemed for their delicate flavor. As a symbol of opulence in old England and New England, turtle soup was indispensable to the ceremonial table. So imagine the excitement that rippled through Newport in December 1752,

Green sea turtle. Courtesy
Roger Hall/www.inkart.net.

when Colonel Samuel Freebody received a giant sea turtle as a gift from his
friend and fellow Newporter George Bressett. As was the custom at the time,
Bressett, who had sailed to the West Indies on business, shipped home a turtle—as well as a cargo of fresh limes—aboard a vessel commanded by Freebody's brother, Thomas. The limes spoiled during the voyage, but the turtle
arrived ready for the kettle. Because of concerns that it might not keep until
after the Christmas holiday, a gala party was planned. Without delay, invita-
tions were sent to more than fifty of Newport's most notable citizens, re-
questing their presence at a "Tyrtle Frolic."

On the afternoon of December 23, guests were transported across Newport Harbor to Fort George, the town's primary defense against sea attack.
Met by a canon salute, the invitees were ushered to the commander's quarters, where they enjoyed a sumptuous meal of turtle soup followed by tea,
English country dancing, and hot toddies.

While turtle parties were popular at any time of the year, it just so happened that Colonel Freebody's coincided with Christmas. In 1971, when
Newporters began planning their first "Christmas in Newport" celebration
to foster the town's noncommercial, historic holiday traditions, everyone
knew that a reenactment of Colonel Freebody's historic "Tyrtle Frolic"
would in time become its own beloved Christmas tradition.

The festivities begin at 6:15 P.M., with a canon salute by the Artillery Company of Newport, the oldest continually active military organization in the country. Mulled wine and cider are served, followed by a mock turtle soup (sea turtles are now protected under the Endangered Species Act) and a hearty buffet of eighteenth-century cuisine. Musicians, playing colonial-era instruments, serenade diners. English circle dancing follows dinner, and the evening ends with guests joining hands and singing "Auld Lang Sine," followed by a rousing cheer, "Welcome Yule!" In keeping with the spirit of community and Christmas goodwill, many events during the now monthlong Christmas in Newport celebration are free of charge; the small donation that is requested at others benefits local charities.

Christmas for the Birds

FROM THE PAGAN practice of animal sacrifice perhaps came a favorite European holiday pastime known as the hunt, during which parties fanned out across the countryside in search of fowl and game to fill huge pies for the Christmas table. It may be that the hunt was a vestige, too, of the mythological Wild Hunt, once widespread across northern Europe, and during which a spectral band of huntsmen, usually led by the sky god, Odin, rode across the night in search of stag and boar. The Wild Hunt reached its frenzied height at the solstice, the longest night of the year.

Another vestige of pagan animal sacrifice was the Hunting of the Wren, a popular Christmastide sport, usually held on Christmas Eve, Christmas Day, or the following day, St. Stephen's Day, across Ireland, England, and France. In pre-Christian times, birds were thought to be messengers from the heavens, intermediaries between this world and the next. For the Druids, no bird was more sacred than the tiny wren, whose song was believed to prophesy the future. The bird's preference for nesting in small, protected crevices led to its being associated with the dark, with the Holly King, and with the waning year. Its sacrifice during the midwinter festival symbolized the killing off of the old year; in its place came the robin, the symbol of the new year.

House wren. Courtesy Roger Hall/www.inkart.net.

By the nineteenth cen-
tury the Christmas "side
hunt" had become a pop-
ular American tradition.
Teams of hunters fanned out
into fields and woods; the
side that brought home the
most quarry—birds and
animals—won.   Such
unregulated and unre-
stricted shooting began
to take its toll on bird
populations, and by the turn
of the twentieth century voices
were being raised in defense of birds
and the preservation of their habitats. One of those
voices belonged to a self-taught ornithologist named Frank
Chapman, whose particular interest was the life history and geo-
graphical distribution of birds. On Christmas Day in 1900 Chapman proposed a new tradition—a Christmas bird *count* rather than a
Christmas bird *kill*. Joined by twenty-seven volunteers in twenty-five locations—including Keene, New Hampshire; Belmont, Cambridge, Boston,
and Winchester, Massachusetts; and Bristol and Norwalk, Connecticut—the
first Christmas Bird Count recorded 18,500 birds and 90 species.

American robin. Courtesy
Roger Hall/www.inkart.net.

Though the Christmas Bird Count predated the National Audubon Society by five years, Audubon now administers the census, the longest-running
database in ornithology, with more than a century of unbroken observation.
International in scope, the Christmas Bird Count, held from December 14
to January 5, is a purely grassroots effort, a living example of citizen action
and citizen science that has enabled conservationists to stay abreast of
trends.

For the tens of thousands of volunteers, from beginners to expert birders,
the count has become a cherished Christmas-season tradition, an opportunity for many to come home to New England, to join field parties made up
of friends and family. The cold rarely deters the volunteers, who, in an atmosphere of friendly competition, remain out all day compiling their data.

One little bird's name on the list surely inspires hope. We still have a vestigial attachment to the humble little bird with the loud and joyful song. The wren, whose gaelic name, *dreoilin,* means Druid bird, reminds us all of the beauty in small things.

Christmas for the Horses

THERE WAS IN Boston many years ago a most out-of-the-ordinary Christmas celebration, a unique way in which the kindness and unselfishness of the season manifested itself. The celebration was called Christmas for the Horses, and it was an opportunity for the public to show its appreciation for the indispensable services the trusty steed had performed for the pioneer, the farmer, the soldier, and the commercial life of the city. Christmas for the Horses was held every Christmas Eve from 1916, through war years and the Depression, into the 1950s. It seemed impervious to time.

It was the cruelty of a "great horse-race" on Saturday, February 22, 1868, "in which two of the best horses of the State were driven from Brighton to Worcester, about forty miles, over rough roads, each drawing two men, and both were driven to death," that convinced George Thorndike Angell—an attorney and a humanitarian—of the need to educate people, especially children, "in the ways of kindness."

Horses' Christmas, Post Office Square, Boston, 1916. Courtesy Massachusetts Society for the Prevention of Cruelty to Animals Archives.

Joined by a number of prominent Boston citizens, Angell founded the Massachusetts Society for the Prevention of Cruelty to Animals (MSPCA), the second society of its kind in the country. It was Angell's successor as society president, Francis Rowley, who began the open-air, free-to-all Christmas celebration for the horses in 1916.

George Thorndike Angell, c. 1880.
Courtesy Massachusetts Society for the
Prevention of Cruelty to Animals Archives.

The event was held at Post Office Square, a site chosen for its proximity to the main arteries of equine traffic and the city's hub, and the scene that first Christmas Eve afternoon warmed the hearts of all passersby. Upon the Angell Memorial Fountain, built in 1912 in part with pennies collected by Boston schoolchildren, a Christmas tree stood tall, colorfully festooned with carrots, apples, bells, tinsel, garlands, and pennants printed with the mottoes "BE KIND TO ANIMALS" and "BLANKET THE HORSE." A reporter noted that throughout the day thousands of spectators viewed the tree and expressed their enthusiastic approval.

By noon the equine guests were arriving at the fountain, and by early afternoon the square was filled with horses and drivers. Members of the MSPCA were kept busy "putting up" dinners consisting of four quarts of oats, a portion of apples and carrots, and several ears of corn. More than one thousand carriage, police, and draft horses lingered over their sumptuous meal that first afternoon—their drivers treated, too, to hot coffee and doughnuts—before resuming their burdens.

The celebration became as much a tradition as hanging a wreath or selecting a tree, as it enlisted public interest in the plight of working horses who, for too long, had trod Boston's streets exhausted, sick, lame, frightened, and abused. On the fifth anniversary of Christmas for the Horses, Francis Rowley wrote: "It is not so much the benefit to the horses as it is a reminder to the people of the worth and faithfulness of the dumb animals. It does the horses good, of course, but they do not remember the food; it is only a meal to them. But the real value of this is to bring home to people the idea of caring for the animals."

Though consideration for Boston's eight thousand working horses waned during the automobile maelstrom of the 1930s, the MSPCA and its devotees persisted. By 1948 television and radio stations were broadcasting the horses' Christmas, and by 1950 the celebration had become part of the City of Boston Christmas Festival. By the mid-1950s, though, Christmas for the Horses had become a victim of the changing times. A moving mass of automobiles had replaced the horses, and without the horses there could be no holiday celebration. George Thorndike Angell's heart would have been gladdened, however, to know that the faithful and unheralded steeds had, for so many years, a Santa to call their own.

The MSPCA continues its work today, its mission—to protect animals, relieve their suffering, advance their health and welfare, prevent cruelty, and work for a just and compassionate society—little changed since George Thorndike Angell chose the path of kindness more than 135 years ago.

THE HORSES' CHRISTMAS

> Come, all you folk of Boston town,
> A pleasant thing to see;
> Look yonder there out in the square—
> The "Horses' Christmas Tree"
> Is loaded down with Yuletide cheer,
> A blessing in their work-filled year.
>
> All you who walk the streets give pause
> And ponder on this sight
> You've often seen—this evergreen
> Tree with its gifts bedight
> For faithful horses, tired and old
> Who daily plod through storm and cold.
>
> They well deserve a Christmas feast
> Who needs one more than they
> Who never shirk the hardest work
> Assigned them day by day,
> And whose reward is, at the best,
> A little food, a few hours' rest?

The hundreds of these toiling beasts
Who will today rejoice
In warming food which they find good
Cannot to thanks give voice,
But every work-horse in the square
Will bless the donors for his share.

Maud Wood Henry, from *Our Dumb Animals*, December 1929.
Reprinted with permission of MSPCA

Index